I0605767

Arctic Ocean

ALASKA

RIA

UNION

• Yakutsk

• Ust' Nera
• Omyakon

Magadan

Bering Sea

Sea of Okhotsk

Troitskoye
Naykhin
Khabarovsk

Lake Baikal

ILIA

LIA

A

Vladivostok

Sea of Japan

J A P A N

JAPAN

Pacific Ocean

INDONESIA

AUSTRALIA

THE WHISPER OF STARS

A SIBERIAN JOURNEY

THE WHISPER OF STARS

A SIBERIAN JOURNEY

PHOTOGRAPHS & TEXT
BY PULITZER PRIZE WINNER
STAN GROSSFELD
FOREWORD BY TOM BROKAW

GLOBE PEQUOT PRESS ★ ★ ★ CHESTER CONNECTICUT

Photographs © 1987, 1988 by the Globe Newspaper Company
Text © 1987, 1988 by Stan Grossfeld

All rights reserved.
No part of this book may be reproduced or transmitted
in any form by any means, electronic or mechanical,
including photocopying and recording,
or by any information storage and retrieval system,
except as may be expressly permitted by the 1976 Copyright Act
or by the publisher.
Requests for permission should be made
in writing to The Globe Pequot Press,
138 West Main Street, Chester, Connecticut 06412.

Library of Congress Cataloging-in-Publication Data

Grossfeld, Stan.
The whisper of stars.

1. Siberia (R.S.F.S.R.)—Description and travel—1981–. 2.
Grossfeld, Stan—Journeys—Russian S.F.S.R.—Siberia. I. Title.
DK756.2.G75 1988 915.7′048 88-16371
ISBN 0-87106-679-3

Jacket photography by Stan Grossfeld
Jacket design by Judy Petry
Photo layout by Stan Grossfeld
Text designed by Kevin Lynch
Additional design and book make-up by Bill Brown
Typeset at Americomp, Brattleboro, Vermont
and Comp-One, New Haven, Connecticut
Separations, printing and binding at Walsworth Publishing,
Marceline, Missouri

First Printing October 1988

For the people of Siberia—the warm glow in a cold place

Foreword

by Tom Brokaw

If there is a common denominator between the peoples of the United States and those of the Soviet Union, it is our abysmal ignorance of each other.

When I finished an interview with Mikhail Gorbachev in an ornate room in the Kremlin's Council of Ministers, just down the hall from a corner office once occupied by Lenin, I asked where in America he would like to visit. There are so many places, he said, I couldn't pick just one. "Aha," I thought, "he's ducking the question because he really doesn't know enough about our country to give an intelligent answer." But then, if a well-informed American were asked the same question about the Soviet Union, the answer likely would be similar. So much of the future will be determined by relations between these two most powerful nations, and yet our knowledge of each other remains so primitive. Astonishing, isn't it?

We look at each other through stereotypical prisms. To many Soviets, the United States is a vast frontier of high crime, low morals, and people who are too rich or too poor. For many Americans, the Soviet Union is a monolithic society of oppressed warmongers whose lives are as gray as a winter sky in Moscow.

As Americans, we know our society is so much more complex and rich than that simple Soviet description. We are inclined to dismiss their view as just another example of the shortcomings of their system. But what of our own ignorance of the U.S.S.R.'s richness and complexity? How do we explain that?

Begin with the basics. Who among us could quickly say, "Of course I know that there are fifteen republics and twenty-one distinct languages within the U.S.S.R. and that it is a country so vast the United States would fit into it twice with room left over for three Alaskas"? Yes, most of us have heard of Moscow and Leningrad. But what about Irkutsk, the Chicago of Siberia, a flourishing city near the shores of one of the world's great bodies of inland water, Lake Baikal?

A city in Siberia? Isn't Siberia one enormous icefield broken up only by primeval forests, fierce beasts, and

A Russian soldier taking pictures

inhumane prisons? Can this same Siberia actually be home to universities, synagogues, ballet, fashion shows, and quaint gingerbread homes? Yes, and Stan Grossfeld shows you that and a great deal more in this compelling account of a journey through Siberia.

The Whisper of Stars lifted me out of Manhattan and deposited me at Grossfeld's side. Through his book we traveled together across this fascinating land so seldom seen and experienced by Westerners. Fair warning, however: This is my kind of trip. My own most memorable journeys have been to the heights of Tibet, to the far reaches of Patagonia, and down the Nile. Creature comforts and conventional attractions don't hold much appeal. Happily, Grossfeld shares the affliction.

I did go to the far-eastern end of Siberia once, but it was with President Gerald Ford and a sizeable entourage of White House officials and American journalists. Our exposure was confined to a remote military base and a long bus ride through the dusk and night to a hastily converted health sanitarium in Vladivostok, the closed Soviet military city on the Sea of Japan. Once President Ford and General Secretary Brezhnev finished their arms control talks, we were whisked out of the country. I didn't even get to see a Gulag. Neither did Grossfeld, but what he did experience makes my little excursion seem like a day trip to the neighborhood fire station.

Grossfeld's greatest challenge was maintaining his patience with his guide, Arkady Kudrya, a "journalist" with Novosti, the Soviet press agency. Mr. Kudrya represents a figure familiar to American reporters working in the Soviet Union. The late Peter Lisagor of the *Chicago Daily News* referred to all of them as "Colonel" because he assumed they had more than a casual tie to the KGB. Even if that is no longer true, Mr. Kudrya does carry on the tradition of his craft. Almost any request is met with a standard response, some version of "Nyet. Is not possible."

To his credit, Grossfeld manages to complete his trip by doing the Siberian version of "take a step, drag Kudrya." Despite enormous resistance he gets to the synagogue; and even though the conversation with the cantor is not very revealing, Grossfeld's determination is impressive. When the Soviets charge him an exorbitant rate for a helicopter charter and then restrict his photography, he throws a tantrum worthy of a Boston Red Sox manager losing a close call at the plate in the play-offs.

Like so many Americans visiting the Soviet Union, Grossfeld finds himself vigorously defending the United States against often-simplistic criticisms. He engages in a

Leningrad: Evening commuters head home.

running debate on the shooting down of KAL 007. His Russian hosts simply refuse to believe the Soviet military made a clumsy, tragic mistake.

Other gaps in the Soviet appreciation of the United States are more understandable. In the most remote reaches of Siberia, ordinary citizens were concerned about the image of their country that came through on the ABC television series "Amerika." Is it any wonder, really? Can you imagine the reaction of many Americans to a program in which we were heartless invaders of the Soviet Union, forcing the population to pay strict allegiance to the worst excesses of our system?

But all of that is only a secondary part of *The Whisper of Stars*. What is especially appealing about this book is that it takes us into the heart of Siberia, a place where it does hover around 30 degrees below zero and colder—for days on end. It takes you to a place where you dine on frozen deer liver, frozen raw horse meat, and perhaps, for those desperate enough to believe it will improve their sexual performance, ground-up deer penis. A place so cold that even the Japanese were defeated when they came to film a commercial about the efficiencies of a Japanese kerosene heater. Yet almost all Siberians we meet in *The Whisper of Stars* seem to be cheery, indeed, proud of their way of life, however primitive or uncomfortable it may seem to outsiders. We may think that if they had an opportunity to leave, they would not tarry at the reindeer station, but that is not the impression that comes through in *The Whisper of Stars*. Another stereotypical impression melts away in the arctic cold.

I was particularly drawn to the Siberian hunter who told the story of pursuing a wildcat with his dog Little Child. The hunter was sure he'd killed the wildcat, only to have it rise up and start for him when his back was turned. Little Child saved the day. That's a tale straight out of early nineteenth-century America. Jim Bridger lives on in Siberia.

As the United States and the Soviet Union enter into what appears to be a new, more productive era of relations, it is especially useful for both sides to have a keen understanding not just of each other's nuclear arsenal, but also of each country's physical and cultural diversity.

The Whisper of Stars is an important book. Through his insight and photographs Grossfeld is an ambassador of understanding and appreciation. I am very grateful that he has given us this book and relieved that he did not freeze to death while searching for the whisper of stars.

Moscow: Tulips at Lenin's tomb

Preface

I went in to see my editor. "I want to be exiled to Siberia," I said.

"What?"

"In the winter. I want to be exiled to Siberia in the winter. There's a mystique about the place and our readers demand that I go."

"You're crazy."

I called the U.S. Army Cold Weather Research Station in Natick, Massachusetts, and spoke to Dr. Murray Hamlet.

"I hate the cold. Hate it. I'm going to Siberia and I need your help."

"What?"

"I hate the cold. I'm going to Siberia and I don't want to die."

"Come over," he said.

I called the Soviet Embassy in Washington, D.C. "I work for *The Boston Globe*, and I would love to go to Siberia to do a story and some pictures."

"It's very cold in Siberia," said Soviet bureau chief Oleg Benyukh.

"I love the cold. Love it."

"Write up a proposal."

A proposal was written; a lunch was scheduled in Washington, D.C., with members of the Soviet Embassy. I drank vodka; they drank scotch. I told them I cared about people, not politics. That there is life in Siberia and I wanted to show it. I showed them books I had produced. Senator Edward Kennedy sent over a letter.

Six months later I got my visa that included visits to places in Siberia where no other Western journalist had ever set foot. Dr. Hamlet took care of the two critical areas—toes and fingers. He lent me a pair of "Mickey Mouse boots" so toasty warm that I spray antiperspirant on my feet to keep them from sweating when it's twenty below. And Army-issue mittens made of wool, fur, and down that I could use when I wasn't operating the camera. *Globe* photo co-op student Judy Dragos reinforced the mittens by sewing in an extra layer of wool. Underneath the mittens are polypropylene gloves. Beneath them are two white super-thin silk gloves. While it may be Siberia on the outside of the gloves, it is always Somalia on the inside.

Actual picture taking would be done wearing just the last three layers. After the pictures are made, the hands go back in the mittens, which are attached to my coat. Just like in third grade.

Long polypropylene underwear, wool pants, a Mt. Everest–tested down–Gore-Tex coat and hood, a NASA survival blanket, handwarmers, and an olive-colored down-filled face mask were all packed. The face mask, although very practical and extremely warm, was only worn once. It bore a striking resemblance to former President Richard Nixon, and Siberian children who saw it were frightened. A step on the scales was equally frightening. The cold-weather gear weighed more than twenty-five pounds.

According to the Soviet Intourist brochure on Siberia, I am overreacting to the climate. "Don't let all the talk about the Siberian frosts frighten you: the winters are cold, to be sure, but by no means unbearably so. In fact, winter is a beautiful season in Siberia: the cities take on a fairy-tale look, the trees are attired in smart lacy gowns, and the snow sparkles in the sun. Siberia is one of those places whose pristine and harmonious beauty makes one wonder at Nature's unlimited creative powers."

Sounds great, but what if my cameras freeze or break? My editors might suggest that I extend my stay indefinitely?

Tom Kennedy, director of photography at *National Geographic*, helped out, getting my equipment winterized by the *Geographic* lab, which removes all fluids that could freeze.

"Watch out when your shutter starts freezing—it slows down and all your pictures will be overexposed," warned Jim Brandenburg, a *Geographic* photographer. "Also, when you are about to go in someplace warm, put the cameras in plastic baggies. Otherwise, they'll stay fogged up for hours."

One camera was kept empty of film during the five-week journey. This camera, dubbed the commie camera, was for all the friendly people that stopped me and asked to have their pictures taken. There are thirty million people in Siberia and that's a lot of film.

But a Polaroid camera provided instant real pictures to give to people—creating instant friends.

The day in February arrived and so did a throbbing toothache. Emergency root-canal surgery was started at Boston University Hospital. It could not be completed. There was a plane to catch.

Moscow: War hero

Soviet health care is free, but with the price of gold being what it is, I didn't want to take advantage of it. With the opportunity of a lifetime ahead, no toothache was going to stop me. I hopped on a jet, transferred at London, and headed for Moscow.

I decided to keep a diary, but I worried that they would read it. Then I remembered what my third-grade teacher in the Bronx had written on my report card. "Stanley's handwriting is illegible. He still does not know how to make some capital letters."

Still, every now and again I would print very neatly, "I love the Soviet Union; the people are friendly," just in case they were looking, which they weren't.

Such paranoia certainly stems from childhood. I remember being instructed to "get under the desk and put your head between your legs" at P.S. 86 in the Bronx during the late 1950s. "The Russians are coming! The Russians are coming!" They never did come, but it still took a good half hour to get the bubble gum that was stuck under the desk out of my hair.

As an enlightened journalist, I know I have been brought up with certain prejudices. There is a heavy feeling about heading to Siberia all alone. It just arrives, in the pit of your stomach, like a letter from the IRS saying you've been audited. The last time I had it was at the Commodore Hotel in Beirut, Lebanon, when the desk clerk inquired in all seriousness if I wanted a room on the car-bombing side or the rocket-grenade side of the building. This journey would have no war, no death, no destruction. This journey would be fun.

On the plane I read that the name Siberia comes from two Tartar words—sib (to sleep) and ir (land). It was settled largely because Ivan the Terrible was trying to extend his empire between 1533 and 1584. He sent Yermak to conquer the native peoples and to force them to pay tributes to him in valuable furs. Ivan gave Yermak special armor to wear on his chest. Legend has it that while crossing a river in battle, the heavy armor drew him down and he drowned.

Today, Siberian furs are still sought after worldwide. Most of the Soviet Union's remaining raw materials are found east of the Ural Mountains in Siberia, and the Soviet Union pours 35 billion dollars a year into getting them out. Siberia is one-third larger than the United States, but has only twelve percent of the population.

My proposal requested going straight to Vladivostok in eastern Siberia and working my way westward. This proposal was made for two reasons. I wanted to spend the maximum time in Siberia at its coldest and keep the

Moscow: Opera at the Bolshoi Theater

Moscow bureaucracy to a minimum. I also requested a visit to Leningrad, just for fun.

My approved schedule dictated just the opposite. First, arrive in Moscow, then visit Leningrad, then back to Moscow, then to Novosibirsk, Siberia's largest city, and on to Irkutsk, where old Russian trade caravans set out for China. Then to Lake Baikal, so deep the Soviets claim it could hold all the water in the Great Lakes. Then, as per my request, travel along the Trans-Siberian Railway to Khabarovsk in the Siberian Far East. From there, north into territory where tourists are not allowed—Yakutsk, in the pole of cold, then 500 miles north to Ust' Nera, where the ground is permanently frozen, and finally to Omyakon, where the coldest temperature of any village was recorded in 1933.

The Soviets also promised visits to places unvisited by any foreigner. I asked them where? "We will tell you when you get there," was the reply. I asked why I could not visit Siberia first via the Far East? "They are not ready for you in Siberia yet," Oleg Benyukh explained. "We must notify them so they can make preparations for your arrival."

I took more than four thousand pictures. None of the film was censored or retouched. The best one hundred are contained in this book.

What emerges on film is a portrait of a warm people in a cold place. They are a good people. I came away with a reindeer coat, an adventure of a lifetime, and a strong message of peace.

Siberia may not be heaven on earth—but it is the opposite of hell, at least in Celsius.

To accompany me on my journey through Siberia, I was assigned a Soviet escort and translator, Arkady I. Kudrya, who once worked for a newspaper in Siberia and is fluent in English. He even spent some time in the United States. He best remembers two things: A black man on a dark street in Washington, D.C., asking him for ten dollars, and a religious demonstration near the Washington Monument. He printed more than twenty black-and-white pictures of the demonstration and placed them in his scrapbook, which depicted visits to Beirut, Libya, and Istanbul. Demonstrations in Moscow are quickly broken up by plainclothes police, sometimes with force. The Washington demonstration obviously fascinated Kudrya; only the belly dancer in Istanbul is as well represented in his scrapbook.

Kudrya is very bright and knows the history, land, and people of the Soviet Union. He loves chess and devours

Moscow: Swimming outside in February

books. He will make sure his guest never freezes. He will help carry luggage, order food, and work eighteen hours a day without complaining. I will even see a tear trickle down his cheek when he relates a tragic story about the whisper of stars. But more about that later.

He also snores, snaps his fingers to get your attention as if you were a Siberian husky, and occasionally claims to be "perhaps too tired" to translate some point the American has made about the Berlin Wall, Afghanistan, Chernobyl, KAL Flight 007, or the Soviet press.

Photographer Dilip Mehta, a Toronto-based photojournalist, had Kudrya assigned to him two months later for the book *A Day in the Life of the Soviet Union.* He remembers Kudrya this way:

"He was not exactly the gung-ho type journalistically to express openness. That's what is worrisome about *glasnost*—not Gorbachev and his policy of openness—but the people down below. You can't get past the palace guards. Every little shot (for the book) was a painful situation.

"We finished shooting late in the day and had to leave early the next morning. I saw a bunch of kids standing next to a bust of Lenin with ghetto blasters. It was a good picture but Kudrya said, 'Time's up. Your twenty-four hours are over.' Five minutes before takeoff he tells me to check in, and then excuses himself to go to the bathroom. When Aeroflot asked me for my passport, I discovered that I left it at the hotel. Kudrya comes back and says that's too bad because all flights are booked for weeks. It was his kind of a joke—he had taken the passport."

Mention the word Siberia and people think of two things: bitter cold and the Gulag, the slave-labor camps. Siberia was once known as the "land of dead souls," a place where Moscow mysteriously disposed of its untouchables. During the nineteenth century, 800,000 souls were sent there.

Joseph Stalin sent between eight and fifteen million people to the camps during the 1930s, then bulldozed all evidence of those killed there. These people worked at construction, mining, lumbering, and other forms of industrial development.

The American Central Intelligence Agency in 1982 estimated that some four million people, of whom ten thousand are political prisoners, are still involved in some form of forced labor.

But the Soviet Intourist brochures breezily say, "Siberia was once a land of prisons, but now, of course, all that's gone."

I had asked Oleg Benyukh just how many remain.

Arkady Kudrya standing in the Hermitage

"How many prisoners do you have in American jails?" he responded. I told him I didn't know, but the figure could be looked up. "Well, we have prisoners in jail, too. Americans think that Siberia is just a big prison camp. That's ridiculous," he said.

On one hand, Kudrya would not honor my request to visit a Siberian Gulag. On the other, he would make sure I wasn't sent to one either.

What kind of a journalist is Kudrya? At my urging he presented me with a manuscript he wrote for *Alaska Magazine* entitled "America's Soviet Neighbors." It begins, "The ship's name was *Inzhener Kazanji*. Evidently because that passenger boat is plying border waters between the ports on the coast of Chukotka, it had the words *CHUKOTKA LINE* written in English across its sides."

Sasha, get me re-writeski! When the story appeared in the July 1987 issue of *Alaska Magazine*, it began. "A biting wind swirled over the endless expanse of white Arctic tundra." The article had been totally rewritten. Only Kudrya's quotes and descriptions based on keen observation were unchanged.

The media is starting to change in the Soviet Union. A local television show had Soviet journalist Stanislav Kondrashov of the Soviet newspaper *Izvestia* as a guest. Kondrashov was reporting on his travels on the Mississippi River with a Soviet group.

Some Americans greeted him warmly and others greeted him not so warmly, he said, as the station showed newsreels of a handful of demonstrators. But he said most people expressed warm feelings toward Soviet citizens.

Kondrashov took questions from the television audience. "Sometimes you journalists report there was an accident in an African country and two people were killed," said a young man, "but something happens here and it goes unreported. That is not serious journalism."

Kudrya, watching the broadcast, observed, "Three years ago you could not have said that on TV."

Another newspaper, the Soviet youth party paper *Komsomol*, reported that there has been a problem with prostitution between the staff and foreigners at Moscow's Intourist Hotel. Kudrya said that this report is also part of *glasnost*.

Once, in an old Siberian hotel, Kudrya knocked on my door. No answer. He bent over and peered through the old skeleton key hole, not knowing I was behind him trudging up the steps. Quietly I shifted onto tiptoe and came right up behind him. "What's going on in there?" I asked.

Together, we maintained a 20,000-mile relationship across the U.S.S.R. that gave me a warm feeling toward the Soviet people but a frustrated view of Soviet bureaucracy.

Russian writer Maxim Gorky once described Siberia as "the land of chains and groans." But the farther we got from Moscow, the more relaxed the people became. Fewer groans and more giggles.

Traveling across Siberia in the dead of winter, comrades, is a jolting study in contrasts. Fly for three hours on a clear night across some of Siberia's nearly four million square miles, and soon you might believe the earth is uninhabited; below lies not a soul, not a light, only blackness. On the other hand, you can go to a world-class ballet in a Siberian city of a million and a half people.

You can ask a dozen people if they've heard of Sinatra or Springsteen and you'll get twelve nyets. But every one of them knows the name of Samantha Smith, the ten-year-old Maine schoolgirl who wrote to Yuri Andropov. She told him she was worried about nuclear war. He invited her to tour the Soviet Union in 1983.

In the Gorbachev age of *glasnost*, the Soviets allowed me unprecedented access in Siberia. But, once there, the challenge was far from over. Sometimes two cars and drivers were hired in case one broke down on some remote frozen river that serves as a highway eight months a year.

This cost a lot of rubles, but it made sense when you read about the Siberian man whose hand was caught under a flat tire when his jack slipped. Before the man could chew off his hand, he froze to death.

We went by helicopter to find reindeer breeders in the *taiga*, the forest which covers most of Siberia. Access to these areas—including Omyakon, which in 1933 registered a world-record-low temperature of minus 96 degrees Fahrenheit—was arranged by the government-approved Novosti Press Agency. The agency sent Soviet journalists along to help translate, guide, and experience the wonders of Socialism every single step of the way.

I don't blame the Siberians for being concerned about their image. They've been getting bad press for several centuries. In fact, an Italian geographical essay in the sixteenth century refuted previous information that Siberia is a "strange land of eternal snows inhabited by a people with beast-like heads and bearlike bodies." The "study" concluded that Siberians are "just like Europeans except they hibernate in the first days of October and only awake in April."

Leningrad: Food store

Moscow: The Bolshoi Theater

The Whisper of Stars

MOSCOW, February 20

Finally, the plane descends, and the stewardess tells everyone to fasten their seat belts. I slug down my drink and suck on the ice cube, which sends a sharp pain into my root canal. I'm heading for the coldest place in the world, and my tooth doesn't like it. Outside, sleet splashes across the window as if someone were throwing snow cones.

To take my mind off my molar, I take notes. But my first entry is, "THROB, THROB, THROB." Unless I get over this damn toothache, only the American Dental Association will read this book. The voyage continues:

"Fog and snow showers swirl around Sherenteyo Airport; finally revealed are rows of neatly stacked houses. Runway is covered with snow. Played 'Back in the U.S.S.R.' on tape player, and the humming of the British Airway landing gear matches the sound effects of the song."

"Welcome to Moscow," says the man who attached the jetway door. I present papers to a uniformed official in a glass cage. He looks at the passport picture, looks at me, repeats this three times. I lift my hat and smile. No smile returned. The baggage-claim area has a mysterious feel to it as guards peer from doorways and darkened corners. A customs official opens one bag containing three hundred rolls of color film. Three hundred rolls of color film in one of the few international airports in the world where photography is against the law! The official calls his superior officer over. My visa tells them I am a journalist, but they can't believe I am going to use all that film. I tell them that I am to be met by Soviet journalist Arkady I. Kudrya of the Novosti Press Agency. I am hoping he is on the other side of the customs door. "Bring him," they say. I go out the door with lenses ranging from an 18 mm wide angle to a 400 mm telephoto draped across my chest. Kudrya is directly in front of the door on the other side. We smile, shake

hands firmly, and I tell him I need his help. He flashes a press card encased in a small red folder, grabs a suitcase, and we head out into the cold.

"If we don't like what you do, we will either kill you or place you in a salt mine," one of the wise guys at Novosti in Moscow jokes. "I'm on a salt-free diet," I reply.

Our exchanges aren't always humorous. On my first full night in Moscow, Kudrya gently pushes my camera down as I am taking a picture of the five-tiered gold Bolshoi Theater. "Not permitted," he says. Furious after watching tourists with Instamatics click away for two hours unmolested, I decide to catch the next flight for Paris.

"My cameras are my hammer and sickle. Don't ever touch them," I say, beginning a ten-minute freedom-of-the-press speech that makes Khrushchev's shoe pounding incident at the United Nations seem like a tap dance. Kudrya at first denies he pushed my hand, then apologizes and offers to pay for tickets out of his own pocket for a return trip to the Bolshoi. He makes good on that promise later.

"Just let us know what you want to see, and we will schedule it. We must get permission first," he says. This becomes the free-world journalists' dilemma. The American journalist wanting to make sure what he sees is genuine likes to be impromptu. The Soviet journalist's job is to keep him on a tight, preplanned schedule. The best stuff, unstaged, unplanned, is not on the schedule.

Hermitage: Snow falling on statue

LENINGRAD, February 21

The search for the whisper of stars begins on a cold February night in Leningrad. It is dark, and the wind off the Baltic Sea drives the snow sideways.

The city is suffering through what are said to be the lowest temperatures since the tragic winter of 1942, when the city was under attack by the Germans. One million of its citizens died during that bitter winter.

"It's too warm for the whisper of stars," says Arkady I. Kudrya, squinting under his fur hat to keep the snow out of his eyes. "The temperature has to be 56. Then when you breathe out you hear 'Shhhhhhhhhh.' That's the whisper of stars. The breath instantly freezes into crystals of ice. Perhaps we will see this in Siberia. It's called habitation fog, and it can be a problem. People in cars can't see where they are going and have accidents."

Kudrya, my Soviet-appointed escort and translator, means minus 56 degrees Celsius (minus 69 degrees Fahrenheit). But in Siberia—where we would spend nearly a month—nobody bothers saying "minus."

One day in Leningrad the day's official schedule takes us to the Winter Palace, where the clock on the fireplace is still stopped at 2:10 A.M. and 20 seconds, the time on November 18, 1917, when the Red Guard troops arrested the bourgeois Provisional Government.

Kudrya says the new Bolshevik government sold paintings from the Hermitage Museum to the United States because it needed gold. These paintings were the start of the National Gallery of Art, he says. (The Soviets actually sold the paintings to Andrew Mellon in 1930–31, according to a National Gallery researcher. These paintings, while part of the original gift by Mellon in 1941 that started the National Gallery, are not considered the cornerstone of the collection.)

We ride the rails of the Metro, which is cleaner and far more efficient than its American counterpart in New York City. It is Sunday, and I suggest a walk in the park. Today is Soviet Army Peace Day, and an admission fee of one ruble is charged at the park entrance. Kudrya says the funds go to the army for "peace." People rent sleds with seats and gently push their children. In the park there is a fenced-in open-air disco. Kids in their teens and twenties are dancing in the snow despite bitter temperatures under twenty degrees. There is an admission fee here, too, and Kudrya wants to leave.

The disc jockey stands on the back of a flatbed truck under the Soviet hammer and sickle seal symbolizing worker and peasant. He's making fun of the people gawking from the other side of the fence. "This is not a zoo," he says. I reach into my pocket for a couple of rubles and pay the cashier. "Rock and roll, Arkady."

She looks pretty dancing on the hard-packed snow. Oblivious to the cold and softly swaying to the music. She is dancing with a girlfriend—not uncommon in the Soviet Union—but she could have been out there all alone. Her cheeks rosy, her eyes closed. The Soviets had already advised me how to stay warm. Lots of warm clothing made of fur, goose grease rubbed on the skin to prevent frostbite. I have a better idea. "Arkady," I say, "Is it okay to ask a woman to dance? I, uh, would like to dance with that woman over there."

Arkady, who up until this point has been steadily reciting V. I. Lenin's life history, suddenly goes into motion and dances over to them. Moments later we are all moving to the fifties classic "Rock around the Clock." Ah, *glasnost*.

Her name is Olga, and when Kudrya tells her our destination is Siberia, she laughs. "My grandmother said to marry someone from Siberia because what they go through gives them good character."

It is the last song, and we invite Olga and her friend for hot tea. On the way she sings an old Russian lullaby, sings it beautifully.

Later she says she loves to go break dancing but "women can't break dance, only men and even then only Negroes are the best." She is angry about a 1987 ABC television series called "Amerika" that depicts the Soviet invasion of the United States. In it the United States is run by evil Soviet agents. "People who put that out should go to jail," she says.

She speaks no English but later Kudrya tells me her story. She has quit teaching and is searching for a new career. She confided she was very much in love with a man once, but he showed little interest in her. She says she took hypnosis so she wouldn't love him anymore. Now he pursues her. "This woman is very unusual," says Kudrya.

The next day Olga accompanies us to a Soviet art show that features a wide range of paintings including a pre–1917 painting of a nude and a Russian version of Huckleberry Finn in tattered clothes on a river. There is a sudden snow squall, but it is ignored by those who wait in line to get in. Once inside I see that Russian art seems more creative and freer than its society.

Olga likes the paintings with colors and light and romance. I lift the camera to eye level to record her favorite. A guard gets upset and sternly says, "nyet." Kudrya flashes his red press folder, but still the answer is nyet.

I am trying to show that the Soviets have a bright culture and talented artists just like the masters— Rembrandt, Renoir, and the other artists represented by nearly three million art treasures exhibited in the Hermitage. I can photograph the great French and Italian paintings, why not the Russian paintings? Gorbachev, the world's greatest public relations man, might agree and change the rules. But a security guard here is like a security guard anywhere else. Nyet is nyet.

That night we go to the Palace of Youth, an elaborate Soviet version of an American "Y." Downstairs, the checkrooms are filled with mirrors, and the young men dressed in Navy uniforms meticulously comb their hair. The young ladies do the same. The club has flashing colored lights but serves no alcohol. It sells berry soda and red and black caviar served on crackers. The music

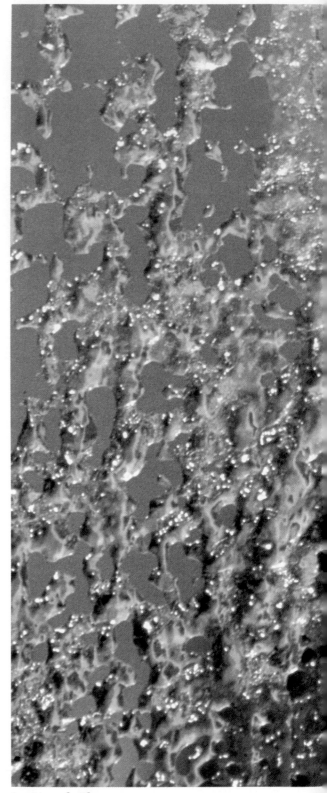

Leningrad: Olga

The Whisper of Stars

is cover versions of old Credence Clearwater Revival tunes. Mostly, boys dance with boys and girls dance with girls. When it's slow dance time, the dance floor empties.

Olga grabs my hand and leads me to the dance floor. Her old boyfriend is there, full-faced, square-jawed in his brown Soviet Army uniform. I don't need an interpreter to figure out she's trying to make him jealous. It works. He sees her, gets flustered, and trips going up the stairs.

Over dinner, Kudrya reads the menu to himself. "Today for a main course I suggest the pork," he says. A fine recommendation, considering it's all they have. However, I'm content with a huge delicious dish of ice cream with chocolate sprinkles.

As is often the case both here and in Siberia, the dinner music is too loud—even at the farthest table. Russian champagne, good although a little too sweet, is served, and there are toasts to peace and to meeting again. The live band plays a Soviet heavy-metal song simulating artillery fire in Afghanistan. Then it launches into "Yesterday."

On the dance floor she is talking softly now in Russian, and I in English, neither understanding the other.

It's snowing and in the teens. The ground crunches underfoot, like walking on Styrofoam. The train station is all lit up; the lights give a warmish glow to the falling snow. Two sleeper cars are loaded for the eight-and-a-half-hour overnight trip to Moscow, stepping off point to Siberia.

We walk toward the train and Olga says goodbye. She will worry about us as we travel through Siberia. Glancing back, I see she's still waving her gloved hand. The scene fades to black and white as the snow gets whipped by the wind and she gets screened out by bundled babies in their mothers' arms and Red Army officers walking like they are being graded on both posture and speed. In Siberia the officers look more relaxed.

Later, over a hot tea served in the berths, I ask Kudrya about writing to her. He says it is okay. No problem. "They may read the first one, though."

I start reading an F. Scott Fitzgerald collection of short stories, purchased in a Leningrad bookstore. It's written in English but has a Russian glossary to explain such English expressions as "the Ritz," "fairway," "wop," "Yankee," and "Harvard." Kudrya suggests we not mention our meetings with the lady of Leningrad. I wonder why not? Is it because she is unemployed and Socialism calls for 100 percent employment? Or is it because *glasnost* hasn't filtered down to the general population? Soviet secrets. Paranoia. We've been brought up listen-

Moscow: Subway entrance

ing to gobs of propaganda about them; they've been brought up listening to gobs of propaganda about us.

Olga did write a long letter back to the States. My reply, transcribed in Russian, returns unopened three months later.

The man who translated her letter is from the Russian Research Center at Harvard. He fled the Soviet Union recently. He thinks Olga was either a KGB spy or someone seeking to leave the country.

MOSCOW, February 25

About an hour out of Moscow, jungle noises are piped through the train's speakers as a wake-up call. The train, smooth and comfortable, arrives on time. The train tracks were built in the late nineteenth century with the blood and sweat of 50,000 serfs. Many were flogged, and thousands of them died during the eight years of construction.

In Moscow, Kudrya completes our bookings with the official state travel agency, Intourist. After several hours the travel agent emerges with our tickets. "This is your itinerary," says Mrs. Pavlova Lyudmila. "We cannot book Yakutia. You can't go there—it's too cold." Yakutia, twice the size of Alaska, is closed to tourists. But Kudrya, who has the patience of Job, irons out the problems. It is one of many he irons out as we travel together.

Kudrya is a member of the Communist Party, one of an elite 6 percent of Soviets. He is in his mid-forties, has silver hair, and lives in a new comfortable apartment on the Moscow River, where he takes me now. To make his apartment look different, he painted a colorful mural of a beach scene in the shower. He collects picture postcards and is against nuclear power. His fourteen-year-old daughter loves the Beatles, especially Paul McCartney's love songs.

Kudrya worked in Siberia as a journalist and is an expert on the Northern peoples living there; in fact, he married one. His wife belongs to the Evenki tribe in Siberia and has written a textbook for them in their own dialect. Kudrya lends me a sable hat—his warmest and most expensive one—and his wife prepares an elaborate dinner, including *stroganina*, a Siberian delicacy of raw frozen fish strips.

Tomorrow we fly to Siberia.

Moscow: A father greets his son at the train station.
(first overleaf) Novosibirsk Airport
(second overleaf) Novosibirsk: New Housing

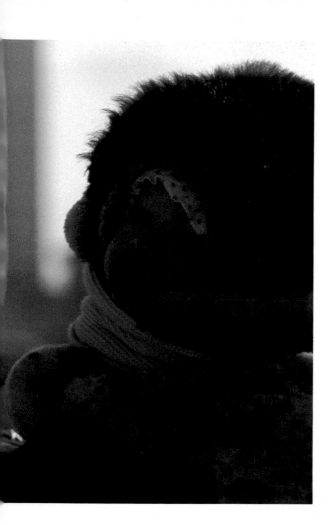

NOVOSIBIRSK, March 1

The Aeroflot jet touches down at 7:20 A.M. in Novosibirsk, 1,800 miles east of Moscow, and taxies past rows of similar jets, their engines covered in burlap, their vents plugged with red caps to shut out ice and moisture. As is the custom, foreigners disembark first, are put on a separate bus, and brought to an empty terminal to await their luggage. In Siberia, segregation of natives and foreigners is sacred.

The main terminal is jammed with people curled up sleeping. Two Red Army soldiers nap on a three-cushioned couch, one with his head on the other's shoulder. All Soviet men must serve at least two years in the armed forces at age eighteen. If they are headed toward Afghanistan, they will grow up quickly.

We are met by a Novosti correspondent named Sergei, who drives us past log cabins and rows of monotonous nine-story concrete apartments.

Housing is an acute problem in Siberia, as in the rest of the Soviet Union. After World War Two, one out of seven Soviets was left homeless, and one hundred million people needed improvements in their housing conditions. But invasion and war left bigger scars than housing shortages. In his own book, *Khrushchev Remembers*, the leader wrote: "I decided that we had to economize drastically in the building of homes in order to build up our defenses."

Much of what was hurriedly built after the war—the so-called Khrushchev housing—is now falling apart.

Novosibirsk's avenues are wide and gray, its storefront decorations sparse and unsophisticated, and its rush hour traffic nonexistent.

This city is Siberia's largest: population 1,500,000. It is the U.S.S.R.'s fifth most populated city, and it is the third largest city in area, smaller only than Moscow and Leningrad.

In 1884 it was called Novonikolaevsk and described by the Russian Geographical Society as "a huddle of huts." In 1893 the Trans-Siberian Railway stretched across the River Ob and into Novosibirsk. At that time there was not a single school in town, and nine-tenths of the population was illiterate. Now the city boasts two-hundred-fifty schools, including fifteen higher-education establishments.

By 1908 the population was 30,000; by 1912 it had doubled. In 1925 the city was renamed Novosibirsk, the "new town of Siberia." By 1934 the population had reached 400,000. During the war, many factories in European Russia were dismantled and moved here. The

population skyrocketed. Intourist now proudly boasts that "Novosibirsk today is an industrial giant, a city of science and culture." It is not, however, the place to go if you are looking for a good pastrami sandwich—the meats are fatty. There are soda and juice machines in various sites around the city but no paper-cup dispensers. A single glass is used over and over. Maybe they figure it's too cold for any germs to live in Novosibirsk.

The sky at daybreak is clear and turquoise blue, then it turns gray. A woman sits on a park bench rocking a bundled baby. There is no wind, less snow here than in Moscow: and the River Ob, which flows north into the Arctic, is not frozen. In July, Novosibirsk has the same average temperature as Paris.

"People from America think that black bears patrol the streets of Siberia," says our driver. The ride to the hotel reveals not a single prison camp nor black bear patrolling the street. In fact, the local television at 8:00 A.M. is showing a Jane Fonda look-alike, with a Princess Di hairdo, doing aerobics on a mat placed on the snow amidst the birch trees.

Exercise is nothing revolutionary. Vladimir Ilyich Lenin, the leader of the Revolution, was reportedly asking for an exercise book when word reached him that the Czar had fallen.

A huge statue of Lenin dominates the plaza on the way to the Siberian Bolshoi ballet. The domed Opera and Ballet Theatre once safely protected selected works of art from the Hermitage, Pushkin, and Moscow collections from the advancing Nazi bombers during World War Two. Inside, the huge coat-check rooms are filled with hundreds of coats, and every available hook has a "Made in Siberia" fur hat hung on it. The theater looks transplanted from ancient Greece, complete with copies of Greek statues. Aphrodite would have loved the two-ton, 13,000-piece crystal chandelier that sparkles before the house lights dim.

Backstage during a matinee performance of *Swan Lake*, director Valerii Brodsky shows the strain of a rough day. "Fourteen of my dancers have women problems, all today," he said.

One swirling swan, a picture of style and grace in front of the curtain, collapsed into a folding chair behind it.

"It's tough for us to get dancers. The stage here is one and a half times bigger than the Bolshoi. Guest dancers come in, take a look around, and leave. Physically, they must be stronger."

I ask permission to climb a steep staircase that goes over the stage to get a different angle. Once there, the angle isn't right. The curtain and some lights are in the

(above) Khabrousk: Up the stairs at the post office
(opposite) Novosibirsk: Lenin's statue outside the Opera and Ballet Theater

The Whisper of Stars

way. I climb one level up and inch along on an old dusty catwalk suspended across the stage, high above the dancers. The lights are hot and the catwalk creaks when I move.

I can see Kudrya, one level below, worrying, wrinkles sprouting on his forehead as he squints to watch me amidst the lights. As I lean out to take the pictures, I notice a rotted plank of wood. I can see the headline now: "Americanski Smash in Swan Lake."

Down the hallway, dancers chain-smoke cigarettes, then hurry back in time to limber up for their next cue. Half-dressed men with layers of makeup play cards, smoke cigarettes until their fingers feel the heat, and tell stories.

We have to leave the ballet before its conclusion because the Soviets have a typed-out schedule of appointments to follow and Fedor Sheffer is waiting. After the unfortunate incident at the Bolshoi Theater, I have given the Soviets a long list of requests for photo subjects. Kudrya advises me to cross out prisons, "because it will make everyone suspicious of you." He says they will try to schedule all other requests, and for the most part, they do.

I had heard that Siberians believe their rugged climate brings long life. Fedor Sheffer, Novosibirsk's oldest man, trim and fit at age ninety-four, remembers capturing Turkish prisoners while serving in the czarist army during World War One. "We were in the 92nd Regiment in Turkey, fighting the Turks and Germans," said Sheffer. "We used the Turkish prisoners to build roads. When word reached us that the Czar had fallen, we were happy. So happy we just left everything there and came home."

He remembers living in czarist Russia as having been "very difficult. We had one big room, one little room, and a kitchen for twenty-one people." Now he lives with his son and daughter in a simple but pleasant apartment where he runs in place in the morning before reading *Komsomol*, the newspaper published by the Young Communist League.

His feelings about Americans? "I'm sure Americans want to live and work in peace."

Reagan? "A toy in the hands of others."

Secret to long life? "You musn't eat much, and always at the same time. I still eat pork fat and potatoes, and I don't eat sugar." His son presents me with a hand-carved sculpture of a fish and tells me to take it to America.

The oldest woman, Anastasiya Ivanova, is 102, but we don't have her address. To find her, we stop at her doctor's house because she knows where Anastasiya

Novosibirsk: Siberian Bolshoi dancers chain-smoke in the hallway between acts at the Opera and Ballet Theater.

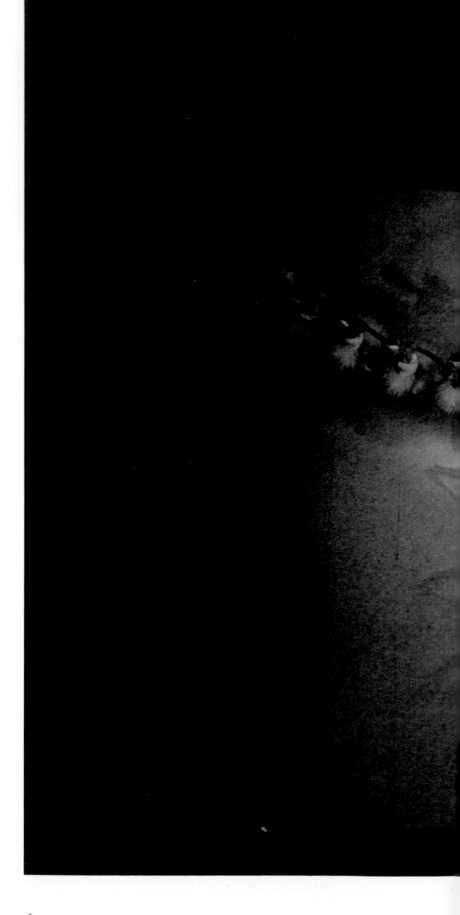

The Whisper of Stars

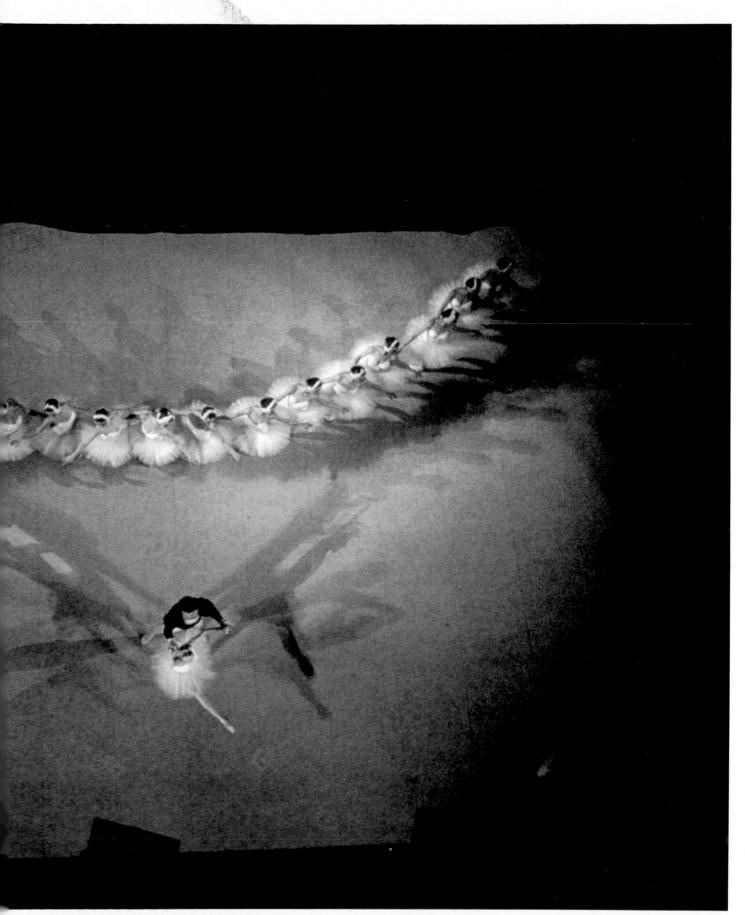

(left) Novosibirsk: A young girl watches the
Siberian Bolshoi perform <u>Swan Lake</u> (above).

lives. The doctor has prepared us a sumptuous four-course meal including sturgeon and cakes. We've already eaten. The doctor's mother hugs me. She says I remind her of her children. She says I am thin and Siberian winters are cold. "Eat!"

She is round and she is proud and she has been cooking all day. What are a few calories for peace between our countries, anyway? I eat. When we arrive at Anastasiya Ivanova's home she announces that she has prepared *blini* for us all. One hundred two years old and still cooking. "I hope you are hungry?" she says, proudly. I shake my head up and down rapidly, figuring the exercise will burn off two, maybe three calories. I used to think they sent people to Siberia to make them talk. Now I know they send you to Siberia to make you eat.

"Mmmm," I pop a whole *blin* in my mouth. Then I yell loudly, "Horror show! Horror show!" Everyone nods approvingly and smiles. The Russian word horasho means "good." With her delicious *blini* and a little caviar and sour cream, we could probably put New York City's Russian Tea Room out of business.

Anastasiya has no aspirations to see the world. In fact, she stays indoors all winter, which is six months long. Her mind remains as sharp as the biting wind.

"I remember many czars, but before the Revolution I remember being very hungry. Now I am ready to die; I have raised ten children and eight have already died. My grandchildren are kind and visit me." Her secret to long life is to "always be kind to people. I never drank and I never smoked and I don't eat beef."

Another group claiming the secret to good health are the self-proclaimed "walruses," Siberia's answer to Coney Island's Polar Bear Club. These men cut ice two meters thick with a saw. Then they jump into the pale green Ob Sea water for twenty seconds to a minute, revolving like spinning tops. The air temperature is 14 degrees F. As one man emerges to towel off in the igloo-shaped wind shelter, he is asked if this ruins his sex life.

"Nonsense," he says. "It makes it stronger."

On the ride back to Novosibirsk, I spot a man on the roof of his log house, shovelling snow as a pale sun peers through the clouds. We stop, hoping to get a candid, slice-of-life photo. Sergei gets out and tries to explain our purpose, but the man leaps off the roof and charges the car. My door is open and I'm pushed in. Arkady grabs the man's wrist and tries to calm him down, but he rants and raves. I hear the word "Amerikanski" in the beginning, but by the end he is apparently commenting

(above) Anastasiya Iranova, 102, the city's oldest woman, offers <u>blini</u> to a guest. (opposite) Novosibirsk's oldest man, Fedor Sheffer, 94, at home with his daughter

(above) Troitskoye: A well-bundled Siberian child
(opposite) Ob Sea: "Walruses" go for their daily dip.

The Whisper of Stars

about our driver's mother. The driver, usually bored by all the waiting around, suddenly seems reborn. He charges out of the car and bumps the man against the door. This form of detente works, and we are off to our next stop: a fashion show.

The occasional rumbling of the walls at the Palace of Fashion was the unmistakable passing of Novosibirsk's subway, an efficient graffitiless bargain at five kopeks (seven cents). It serves as a drumroll for the new fashions.

The fashion show features students and models displaying stylish fur coats on a runway that could have been in Paris or Milan. Siberians are becoming more fashion conscious. The move is away from the drab, colorless uniforms. Women put sparkles around their eyes, and the biggest department store offers 40 percent off on flimsy red negligees.

Imported blue jeans were once available only on the black market, but now they can be purchased in stores at the royal rip-off rate of 100 rubles (about $150); Soviet-made jeans cost half that.

A visit with an English class of Novosibirsk Teachers Training College reveals a real curiosity about America.

(below) Novosibirsk: Siberian fashion show
(opposite) Karakan Forest: Snow removal

The dozen students—mostly women—were asked to write a message to be delivered to the American people. Here are the replies:

"Human intercourse is the best happiness in the world, intercourse between our nations is happiness too." —Vazhenina Irene

"You know, Stan, unfortunately sometimes there is a lack of understanding between American people and Russian people. But it's really a great thing that there is a wish to understand." —Natasha

"We do like American people, American songs; we would like to be friends. Siberian winters are cold, but our hearts are warm." —unsigned

"I wish good luck to you all (I mean all American people). Let's be good friends, then everything will be okay." —Olga Svetlana

"People of the U.S.S.R. want to live in peace with all countries of the world. Let's live in peace!" —unsigned

"You're a nice boy, Stan. We'll be glad to see you again in our city. We want to be friends with Americans and meet each other more often." —Pavilenko Oksans, Shrajber Andre

The students are a little shy but charming. The table is filled with sturgeon, caviar, cakes and cookies, a local berry juice, tea, but no alcohol. "We look down on drunkenness," one student says, echoing a Gorbachev reform.

"We are not bored," says another. "We have six theaters here. We go out into the woods and pick mushrooms and berries."

They sing songs for their guest, including "Old Mac-Donald Had a Farm" and "Puff, The Magic Dragon." I don't have the heart to tell them that the latter song is suspected of being about smoking marijuana.

The teacher, Zoya Essebva, was evacuated from Leningrad during World War Two, more commonly referred to as The Great Patriotic War. "We took off and the Nazis hit our plane. I was a little girl, but I can remember my mother turning gray," she recalls.

NOVOSIBIRSK, March 3

Snow is falling—a spring snow, the Siberians say, because it is wet. Winter snows are dry and hunters have twenty different terms to describe the different qualities of the snow.

Novosibirsk looks better in snow, especially the huge statue of Lenin. Ninety years ago to the day he passed through Novosibirsk en route to exile. He described the

(above) Novosibirsk: Students at the teacher's college
(opposite) Ust' Nera: Schoolboy and Lenin poster

The Whisper of Stars

Siberian countryside in a letter mailed to his mother from here.

"There are no farmhouses, no towns, villages are few and far between, the woods are sparse, nothing but steppe, snow, and sky."

Surrounding Lenin are five statues symbolizing the driving forces of the Revolution: on his right, a worker, a soldier, and a peasant; to his left, a youth bearing a torch and a girl with a sheaf of grain.

Later, when the snow stops, a Red Army soldier tries to steal a kiss from his girlfriend at the Heroes of the Revolution Memorial Park. The soldier spots a foreigner approaching and the couple vanishes behind a mural wall depicting Socialist Revolutionaries with raised arms. I see a huge boulder with a Statue of Liberty–like torch—with only the arm and torch breaking out of the ice. Underneath lie the bodies of 104 Bolsheviks killed during the Civil War in December 1919.

History lesson over, it's time for science. We head for Akademgorodok, the "Academic City" seventeen miles south, in the geographical center of the Soviet Union. This is home to 3,000 scientists and 10,000 technicians. It was built in virgin woods by 8,000 workers—mostly teenaged boys and girls who volunteered in 1957. The project took seven years to complete, but the rewards have been great. Space-exploration research, Soviet nuclear defense projects, interpretation of ancient Mayan writings by computers—are all done here. There is also a computer capable of performing 100,000 mathematic operations a second. In the right hands, it could eradicate algebra homework from the face of the earth and make the world a better place to live.

The roads leading there are icy and empty.

In an operating room a twelve-year-old boy lies unconscious. His body is covered with ice. Even his outstretched arm has a chunk of ice placed in the palm of his hand. A team of doctors and nurses monitors his body temperature. He has come from Yakutia, more than a thousand miles away to the northeast, to have a heart wall repaired. When the boy's body temperature drops to 78 degrees F, his heart can be stopped safely for at least ninety minutes without any damage, according to Professor Eugenij Meshalkin, director of the Research Institute of Pathology and Blood Circulation in Akademgorodok.

"The purpose of the ice is that everywhere else in the world they use an artificial pumping system with complex equipment and transfusions of blood," says the seventy-year-old Meshalkin. "We perform the same thing without the use of it. It's a lot cheaper, and the

Akademgorodok: professor Eugenij Meshalkin and surgeons successfully perform open-heart surgery without anesthesia. The boy's heart stops when his body temperature drops to 78°F.

The Whisper of Stars

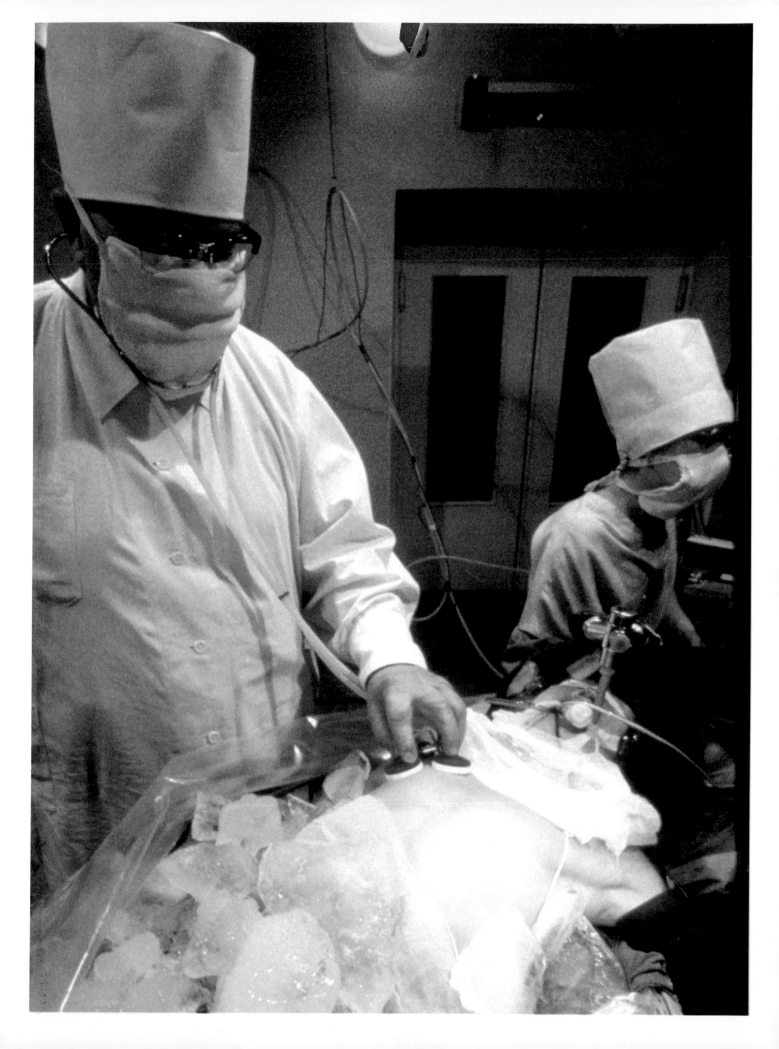

mortality rate is less because donors' blood can cause bad consequences. And a pump is not a real heart." On the wall in his office is the obligatory Lenin portrait, plus a portrait of General Secretary Mikhail Gorbachev. The wine colored birthmark on Gorbachev's forehead has been retouched.

While the youngster cools down, Meshalkin takes us to a projection room and shows a video of open-heart surgery. "This is a revolutionary technique I would be happy to demonstrate in America," he says proudly. The video is so graphic with its super close-ups that I'm beginning to feel like a capillary. Thankfully, it ends but Meshalkin puts on another one.

He explains that he left Moscow twenty-seven years ago. "I don't miss Moscow and all its traffic." He performed his first heart operation during World War Two when "two soldiers were carried in and I didn't have time to be scared" and his first experimental heart operation in 1948. Under his supervision, the hospital has performed 10,000 heart operations in the last ten years. In two other operating rooms, a man and a woman are cooling down for their open-heart operations.

The second video is over and Meshalkin pops in a third cassette. Professor, have a heart. Moments later we are notified that the operation is about to begin. I opt for the overhead viewing site because it is the farthest away from the action.

The operating room is very bright. Eight or nine doctors and nurses cut and sew. Whatever blood spurts out is collected and put back in the lad. After about ten minutes someone asks if I am finished taking pictures. The bright lights were put on for photography, and the kid could thaw if they aren't turned off soon.

Out in the cold, the birch trees grow for miles and miles. On our return to Novosibirsk, we pass some log houses nestled among them. Kudrya doesn't want the gingerbread log houses photographed because they have no running water or bathrooms and are symbols of the past. I explain that they are picturesque and would command a fortune if located on Martha's Vineyard, off the coast of Massachusetts.

During a walk through Novosibirsk's library, an open window gives a decent overall view of a log-cabin neighborhood. I stop and take a picture. Kudrya, walking behind me, looks out the window, just like he watches everything else I point a camera at. He is not happy, later scolding me for absentmindedly whistling in the five-million-volume library. The collection boasts rare ancient Arabian and Abyssinian manuscripts on palm

Novosibirsk: The crew of an Aeroflot plane that crashed in 1984 are buried together.

leaves and literary works of the fourteenth century on parchment.

In 1750 a description of the Siberian Kingdom was published for Empress Elizabeth. Entitled *Royal Academy of Sciences Description of Siberia,* it is believed to be the first written history of Siberia.

"The majority of the people who live in Siberia are illiterate . . . and are made up of the Tartars who live in fear in scattered areas. The real story of Siberia starts with the time of the reign of Ghenghis Khan which dates back to the 13th century after the birth of Christ."

The *History of Siberia,* published in 1774, said that "When the Russians conquered Siberia they did their best to protect the Eastern front from the Tartars but even in spite of that, most of it is empty. Although the place is very cold the air is very clean and pure. People would have lived for a very long time if not for the drinking which stopped their lives."

At a geological museum the guide uses a pointer on a map of Siberia to show its wealth of gas, coal, diamonds, and gold. There is a legend that when the earth was being created, God took all the goodies, the diamonds and gold, and sprinkled them safely in Siberia where no one could reach them. Now the Soviet Union pours 35 billion dollars a year into getting them out.

Our guide claims that Pope John Paul ordered a blue and white marbled mineral called charoit, discovered in Yakutia, for his tombstone at a price in excess of one million rubles ($1,350,000 U.S.). Vatican sources officially refused comment but unofficially thought this was funny.

Burying the dead in the dead of winter is a problem. Grave diggers spread coal on the burial plot and then pour benzine over it. The coal burns overnight and softens the ground enough to dig. A visit to a cemetery revealed photographs of the deceased on each tombstone. A gypsy leader had a life-sized monument as his tombstone, and a crew of Aeroflot flight attendants who all died in a plane crash were buried side by side. Their smiling faces in uniforms gave an eerie chill to an already chilly day.

Karakan Forest: Fox hunting, Siberian style

The Whisper of Stars

NOVOSIBIRSK, March 4

A 5:45 A.M. wake-up call. Outside it is dark, with not a soul on the streets. It is snowing, and the snowflakes hypnotize like twinkling stars as they head into the high beams. The highway has but one lane, and after an hour of darkness, tail lights appear ahead. Could it be someone stranded? The spill of the high beams illuminates a green truck, and as we speed past it, there sits a Soviet tank at the side of the road. The turret is open and there is just a glimpse of an open-mouthed soldier. In reality, more like a kid with a big toy amidst the swirling snow in the middle of nowhere. "Don't worry," Sergei says. "They are not here on your account. We have a great army and they have to be somewhere. They are probably here on maneuvers."

After a two-hour drive, we are welcomed at the log-house headquarters of Genady Efimov, chairman of the Hunters' Society of Novosibirsk. He is in charge of 3.5 million acres of land, roughly the size of Massachusetts and Connecticut combined. Efimov organizes hunters' work, provides licenses, sells furs and meats to the state, and takes care of the forest. He has a gold toothy grin and wears a brown polyester suit as he drives his jeep through the Karakan Forest. It is bitter cold out, but he says we will have trouble seeing elk this morning "because it is too warm, they will be lying down." A visit to the outhouse is one reason to be thankful it is still well below freezing. Hunting season is over but—unbeknownst to me—he has decreed a one-day holiday to show the American how the Siberian hunts. A fox, outfoxed into thinking hunting season is over, and two hares are the victims. We meet a hunter named Boris, who wears a white suit that blends into the snow and birch trees. He has skis that have strips of elk fur on them, so his feet won't slip backwards. His dog nips at the dead fox.

Back at the cabin a feast is being prepared by two women who are accountants for the Hunters' Society. They have prepared fish, chicken, and *pelmeni*—a Peking ravioli stuffed with elk meat and served with sour cream or butter. It is delicious. The women never join us at the table and remain in the kitchen all day, despite my strenuous invitation. They have hand-rolled more than 500 of the bite sized *pelmeni*, but they don't get to enjoy them. Raisa Gorbachev may be liberated; these women are not.

Genady prefers to talk about the virtues of elk meat. "It is very low in calories and cholesterol." He also says that Siberian grain is exported to Italy, where the

Near Novosibirsk: Winter hibernation for iced-in ships

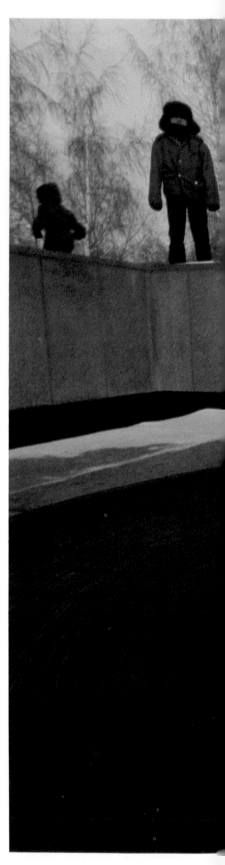

(above left) Novosibirsk: Some of the 33,000 names of local men killed in World War Two. (left) High-school honor guards are replaced every fifteen minutes at the Eternal Flame (above).

Italians make semolina from it. There are the standard, although sincere, toasts with straight vodka to peace and friendships between our countries. A frozen bumble bee appears to be preserved forever in a window that gets no sunlight. It is time to go, and one of the hunters presents a gift of antlers. "Bring them to America," he says.

Nearby there is a house that has a flag painted on it along with the words, "In this house lives a participant of the Second World War." Another sign reads, "Here lived a man who went off to war and never returned." The signs are there to remind young people to take care of the victims of war. We make an unannounced stop, and a seventy-year-old man who had been shoveling snow comes over and tells his life story in thirty seconds.

"I took part in the Battle of Kursk—Battle of the Tanks [the greatest land battle in history, in which 3,000 tanks participated and 25,000 Nazis were killed]. I killed many Germans and received many medals. I was born in this house, my father lived in it, and I would like to stay in it till the end. The war took much of my health." He stands by the end of his picket fence and leans on his shovel and watches us drive away. I turn around and watch him through the rear window until he blends into that fence.

The road back to Novosibirsk is partially across a frozen lake that reduces a 186-mile drive to 87. A motorcycle with a sidecar attached to it zooms by. We track it down. How can anyone ride a motorcycle in such bitter cold?

"It is spring," says the driver.

Soviets are obsessed with World War Two, the result of having lost at least twenty million people. Reminders are everywhere. This afternoon we visit the Novosibirsk Monument of Glory, which lists in bronze the names of 33,000 local war dead.

The changing of a goose-stepping school honor guard, armed with rifles, occurs every fifteen minutes during the day at the Eternal Flame. The goose step resembles a place-kicker booting a field goal in slow motion. It is disturbingly similar to the way the Nazis marched.

Behind the honor guard a side door to a truck carrying freshly baked loaves of thick Russian bread pops open. The driver stops and rushes to close it as the steam pours out into the bitter cold.

Outside the Palace of Sport fur-hatted Siberians peer into the windows of the swimming pool. The complex includes a movie theater that shows Fellini films, an ice rink where children put on skates as soon as they can walk, and a gymnasium where some pleasantly plump women have just finished an aerobics class. They wear

Novosibirsk: At the Palace of Sport, parents watch their children swim.

The Whisper of Stars

ill-fitting, one-piece swimsuits with clashing homemade, hand-knit stockings.

In the basketball arena a team from the Trans-Siberian Railway passenger crew is warming up to face a Trans-Siberian cargo crew team. All the fantasy basketball games I've had as a kid bouncing a ball in a driveway have been against the Soviet Union. Now here they are in the flesh. I ask to take a shot. Both teams stop shooting and the arena gets quiet. In my mind, this is for the gold medal, three seconds on the clock, and the U.S.S.R. leading 91–90. I dribble twice to the top of the key and take an arching jump shot that rattles around the rim and in. Kudrya has a little conference and I am invited to play for the cargo team. Russian hospitality. The game is sort of a Siberian rugby. One player puts his head down and dribbles until someone practically tackles him. In the first minute of the game, I feel my heart pounding wildly. Louder than the sound of the basketball bounced on the floor.

I leave my man unguarded, sneak up behind the opponent dribbling the ball, and steal it cleanly. The ref blows the whistle and the temptation is to argue the call. Instead, I smile. It's ridiculous to argue. The ref speaks no English, and the rules could be different here, like argue a call and work a year in the salt mines.

My teammates, who usually run from one basket to the other, waiting for rebounds, are surprised when I hit them with passes. So surprised that the ball often hits their hands and rolls out of bounds. By the second quarter they are catching those passes and getting easy lay-ups. The bench and the handful of spectators are applauding. We jump ahead by ten points. With the seconds ticking down just prior to halftime, I cut for the basket, and one of my comrades hits me with a perfect pass for an easy lay-up. The whistle signals halftime, and my new teammates swarm around me and shake my hand. I ask one of them if he ever heard of Larry Bird. The man starts chirping.

When I find out that a small, dour-faced man has been benched so I can play, I decide it is time to go. Kudrya, eager to please, tells me I am high scorer with six baskets. It's a reminder of the need for verification between the United States and the Soviet Union. I know I have scored only three points.

A young male dancer does his exercises.

AKADEMGORODOK, March 5

It's bitter cold—4 degrees F—and there's a haze around the city that the sun can't seem to burn through. Aleksci

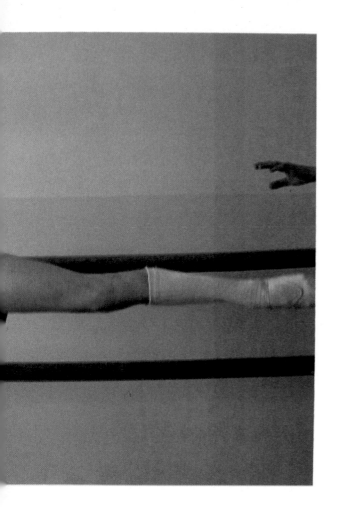

Bogachev is sitting in his office complaining bitterly about the weather "There are very strong winds, and when they blow it is very hard to walk. The winds are caused by the skyscrapers." Bogachev, as it turns out, is referring not to Siberia, but to Boston, where he just visited.

"At M.I.T. there are sculptures to block the winds. In Novosibirsk there are winds, but not as strong as that." Bogachev is director of the specialized School of Physics and Matter in Akademgorodok and has helped arrange a student exchange with Phillips Academy in Andover, Massachusetts. "America has everything. We still lack cafes and restaurants where people can spend free time and utility services like shoe repair or hairdressers. Americans are very open. Attending classes there made me feel like I was in my own school."

At a school for ballet students in Novosibirsk, an impromptu stop in a classroom finds them studying the United States. "What do you think of Negroes?" one boy asks. Many Soviets have seen newsreel footage of blacks being hosed and beaten from the civil rights marches of the sixties. Some even think that blacks are still slaves.

Scene of the day: A woman and a man, both about sixty years old, get out of a cab. The woman, who carries a package, says something harshly to the cabdriver. He opens the door, reaches out, and shoves her. With a flick of the wrist she uppercuts the cabby with her package. The startled driver, reeling from the punch, shuts the door and drives away. The woman grabs her companion's arm and climbs up on the sidewalk.

Getting married in the Soviet Union is twice as easy as it is in the United States. Instead of the wordy "I do," all you have to say is "da." The Palace of Weddings is two stories high, has a circular stairway and a marble room, and usually holds twenty-four weddings a day. The ceremony starts off with a worn record playing Tchaikovsky's "Piano Concerto No. 1" and ends with a bit of advice from the deputy governor, who uses a pink pointer to tell the bride and groom where to sign. "Life is very difficult, but even in happiness, don't forget your parents." This particular marriage between Andrei Lebedev and Natasha Boskonzhieva is a mixed one. He is Russian, she Yakut. No matter; both mothers cry. The ceremony takes five minutes, and the wedding photographer has his huge photo floodlights permanently installed in the room. When the newlyweds leave, five teenaged Red Army soldiers have just finished shoveling a path to their car. Andrei carries his bride to the car, decorated simply with two strands of crepe paper. Their next stop is the Monument of Glory, where they offer flowers. Our guide tells us that at traditional weddings the guests throw money on the floor, "usually enough for a furniture set. The bride gathers the money because that symbolizes that she can manage the household."

One month before the ceremony, the couple comes to the Palace of Weddings to fill out the marriage applications and receive instructions entitled "To those getting married":

> A simplistic, trite or unthinkable approach to marriage and the family can lead to distant and unsuccessful marital relations, which are usually easily ruptured to the detriment of the life and future of the couple's children.
>
> Dear friends, before taking this important and responsible step in your lives, make sure once again that you are ready to found a family and take on the lofty civil and marital obligations toward each other and your future children.

On the ceremonial day of the wedding, the bride and bridegroom, with their parents and guests, come to the Palace twenty to thirty minutes before the wedding. The best man and bridesmaid help the couple out of the car, open the doors of the Palace, and accompany them into the reception hall allocated to them. The newlyweds will stay at the Palace for nearly an hour. During that time, documents will be formalized, photographs taken, and the bride receive her indemnity check for her wedding ring.

I notice a page about sexual hygiene—Siberian style. I nonchalantly grab it and start folding it up. Tonight is going to be a steamy night with the pocket Russian-English dictionary. I feel like a thirteen-year-old who has just sneaked his first copy of *Playboy* into the house. Siberia's magazine racks have no *Playboy*, no *Penthouse*, no capitalist sexual exploitation. The magazine covers here have tractors, or Gorbachev, or hydroelectric plants, or cosmonauts on their covers. What's written on this sexual hygiene page? Sad to say, that remains one of Siberia's mysteries. A woman in the office comes over and pulls the paper out of my hand as if it were a list of secret Soviet military installations. She says nothing but offers a stare normally reserved for child rapists.

Divorce rates in the Soviet Union are high—70 percent of all marriages break up within a decade. A twenty-seven-year-old divorced woman says that she

Novosibirsk: Newlyweds leave the Palace of Weddings.
(overleaf) Novosibirsk: A shopper expresses delight at finding fresh tomatoes at the market.

The Whisper of Stars

meets men at dances, through friends, or through families. "Of course, meeting through families is the worst."

Back at the hotel it is time to pack. Our flight east leaves for Irkutsk late that night. Each floor of the hotel has a caretaker who handles guests' keys, sends the laundry out, brings guests tea and mineral water, and keeps an eye on activities. Tonight she offers tea with crackers and homemade blackberry jam. She is eager to talk because she misses her son who is in the Red Army.

I go for a walk alone. There is only a short line at a bakery, which serves tea or juice and chocolate cupcakes or cheese sandwiches. I spot the same brand of cookies I was served in the Karakan Forest. My hosts were treating me first class—the cookies are the most expensive in the store.

At a department store there is a two-line system: Pay at the cashier, and then present your receipt to pick up your goods. There is a flurry of activity as a new Soviet perfume has arrived. Middle-aged Soviet women crowd into that corner with reckless abandon, like they're on the Soviet Olympic hockey team, down a goal, and the puck has headed into the corner with twelve seconds left. A quick whiff, and it's decidedly Paris—Paris with just a hint of Perth Amboy, New Jersey.

The next department—Lenin busts—is deserted. In a food store the meat selection is poor and mostly fatty. At a liquor store, lines—and faces—are long. The daily opening of liquor stores is delayed three hours, and the price of vodka has doubled in the last year. Soviet officials blame excessive drinking for the decrease in the male life expectancy—from sixty-seven to sixty-two over the last twenty years.

The wide avenues here are quiet, because few have automobiles. By midnight the streets are deserted.

The procedure at Novosibirsk Airport is typical for a foreigner. Wait for flight in a separate terminal. Take a separate bus to the jet where men, women, and children are pushed out of the way to let the foreigner board.

The plane is unheated, and everyone sits bundled in his coat. I am content to listen to a tape on my Walkman and read the *Moscow News*. A man seated behind me starts complaining about something and calls for a stewardess. The man, husky and red-faced, is upset with me. He thinks I am an American spy and am tape-recording Soviet secrets.

Kudrya calms him down, and I offer the man the opportunity to listen to the "spy tape," which features Elvis Costello singing "The Angels Wanna Wear My Red Shoes." He declines.

Aboard an Aeroflot jet, a youngster stays bundled up.

The Whisper of Stars

Unlike flights in America where carry-on luggage must be under the seat or secured in the overhead rack, flights here are a luggage free-for-all. Dog rights have come a long way since the Soviets launched a dog named Laika into space on a one-way exploratory ticket in November, 1957. Now they are carried on board without having to ride in those plastic animal suitcases that make their owners so nervous.

In the next seat is a woman with red-tinted hair and a heart-shaped face. Her name is Lena, and she says she is an engineer in Novosibirsk and is heading home to Irkutsk for Woman's Day celebration. Workers enjoy free travel and vacations of up to forty-two days as incentive to live in Siberia. Lena spends part of the trip listening to Western music on my Walkman. She asks to hear one song a second time. Asks for the name of the song in Russian. It is called "Ogón," or, as Bruce Springsteen sings it, "Fire."

A Red Army soldier gets up four times to push luggage into the overhead rack. It falls on him each time; finally he sits with it in his lap. We arrive in Irkutsk at 3:15 A.M. Lena tells us we must not fail to visit Lake Baikal, the deepest lake in the world. "The berries that grow along the lake are the size of your fist," she says.

IRKUTSK, March 6

It is 4 degrees F when we arrive in Irkutsk, the Chicago of Siberia (population 550,000). This city is less cosmopolitan and more charming than Novosibirsk. It is a city renowned as a major supplier of furs to world auctions.

A young Joseph Stalin was banished here in 1903 and escaped a year later. In the mid-seventeenth century the Czar sent an envoy here in hopes of collecting tributes. The local Buryat tribesmen didn't see a need for taxation, nor a need for representation. They murdered the envoy, then held out for twelve years before the Russians established a fort here.

Explorers from Irkutsk settled parts of both California and Alaska. They were governed from a stately gothic building that still stands here. It's called the White House.

In April of 1806 a Russian ship, the *Juno*, sailed into what is now San Francisco. Russian Count Nickolai Rezanov came to negotiate a trade agreement, but instead he left his heart there, a full 150 years before

Tony Bennett sang the song. The reportedly handsome and aging widower fell in love with a Spanish *coman-dante*'s beautiful daughter. It didn't bother him that she was fifteen years old—this was California. The Count's plans were to return to St. Petersburg, propose that the Czar send him to Spain to negotiate a treaty, and then marry Concepcion. While en route to the capital he caught a fever and fell off his horse.

Concepcion didn't receive word of his death for thirty-six years. She remained faithful to his memory and joined the Third Order of St. Francis, devoting the rest of her life to caring for the sick and the poor.

In 1812 the California fur-trading settlement of Fort Ross was established on a bluff overlooking the harbor. The Russians sold the settlement to John A. Sutter in 1841 for $30,000 plus some flintlock muskets that were captured when Napoleon was forced to flee Moscow.

Today Irkutsk has four theaters, several cinemas, a philharmonic, a planetarium, and a cycling track. Its woods boast brown bears and red deer, and the city has protected some of its old wooden houses with the fanciful carvings and declared them to be historical landmarks, despite Arkady Kudrya's feelings about them.

Scene of the day: There is a flurry of activity on Karl Marx Street. People scurry, like ducks all heading toward bread tossed in a pond, for a glimpse of something new. A man has set up a table with small dirty carrots on it. With a corkscrew-type Vegematic, he is burrowing strips. You don't need a translator for the sales pitch— "It slices, it dices."

I have made several requests to visit a synagogue. Many Jews are trying unsuccessfully to leave the Soviet Union, so this is a sensitive request. After one particularly annoying answer, "we don't know where the synagogue is," I resort to hardball. "Let me write a story the way you might," I said. "An American Jew was denied the right to practice his religion while in Siberia."

The next day in the synagogue a man with a white hat and apron mixes flour and water together. He kneads the dough and then brings it to an electric roller—a sort of rolling pin with spikes. This cuts in the small indentations that will prevent the dough from burning. Then the dough is spread on a twelve-foot-long table, cut in strips, placed on a long wooden stick, and fed into a birch wood-fired oven. By the time the chef says, "The secret

The Whisper of Stars

Irkutsk: Mordeccai Ben Rubin Levenzon carries the Torah past a wall and a sign referring to those who died in World War Two.
(first overleaf) Irkutsk: Making matzoh in the synogogue
(second overleaf) Irkutsk: A Jew in prayer.

to good matzoh is a very hot oven. We start heating ours the night before," the matzoh is done.

On the other side of the wall, a service is in progress with a dozen men. The stained-glassed synagogue looks no different here than in any other city. The names of war dead are behind the worshippers, written on a wall with a sign in English saying, "no one is forgotten."

One man in his nineties says that he was wounded during World War One on the German front. He says he was placed on a train heading toward St. Petersburg. Two doctors on the train saw him and said, "You are not Russian." He said he was Jewish, and they told him he had no right to be on the train. "The Russian daughter of Czar Nicholas, Tetayana Nicholiana, demanded that I be removed from the train," he said.

Mordeccai Ben Rubin Levenzon, the synagogue's cantor, answers quickly when asked if there is religious persecution in Irkutsk. "In this city no one wants to leave. No one interrupts our services." Briefly we are alone and I ask again, this time using the one word of Yiddish I know, "Tsorus?" The word means aggravation and Levenzon again says no. Twice we have been to this synagogue, and neither time has the rabbi been here. "His wife is ill," Levenson said. I am given a package of matzoh big enough to build a two-lane highway across the Red Sea. "Take this to America," he says.

Downtown a big brown bear stands in the plaza, paw extended toward shoppers. The bear is stuffed, and 7 rubles, 40 kopeks ($11) gets you three color photos with the bear. The photographer taking the pictures tells the people to come back in a week for their prints. A capitalist tells him about the wonders of Polaroid, and his eyes get bigger. When the capitalist mentions the cut-out life-sized photographs of President Reagan that people pose with, the photographer grins ear to ear. Head for hibernation, big black bear; make room for Gorbachev and Lenin.

Nearby, under the obligatory poster of Lenin in the Irkutsk fur factory, Clara Vetohena picks up water-rat skins, inspects them, and tosses them into one of ten different quality bins. There are 6,000 water-rat skins in front of her in this largest fur factory in the Soviet Union. Vetohena, her black jacket covered with rat lint, said she's not bored, "because no two water rats are the same." Put twenty dead water rats together, and you've got yourself a water rat coat.

Vetohena's wages are 20 percent higher than those for a similar job in Moscow would pay, a reward for working in Siberia. Some jobs, like outdoor railroad workers, pay double. She makes 200 rubles a month and has two

Irkutsk: Stuffed bear and child
(overleaf) Lake Baikal: Steam bath

The Whisper of Stars

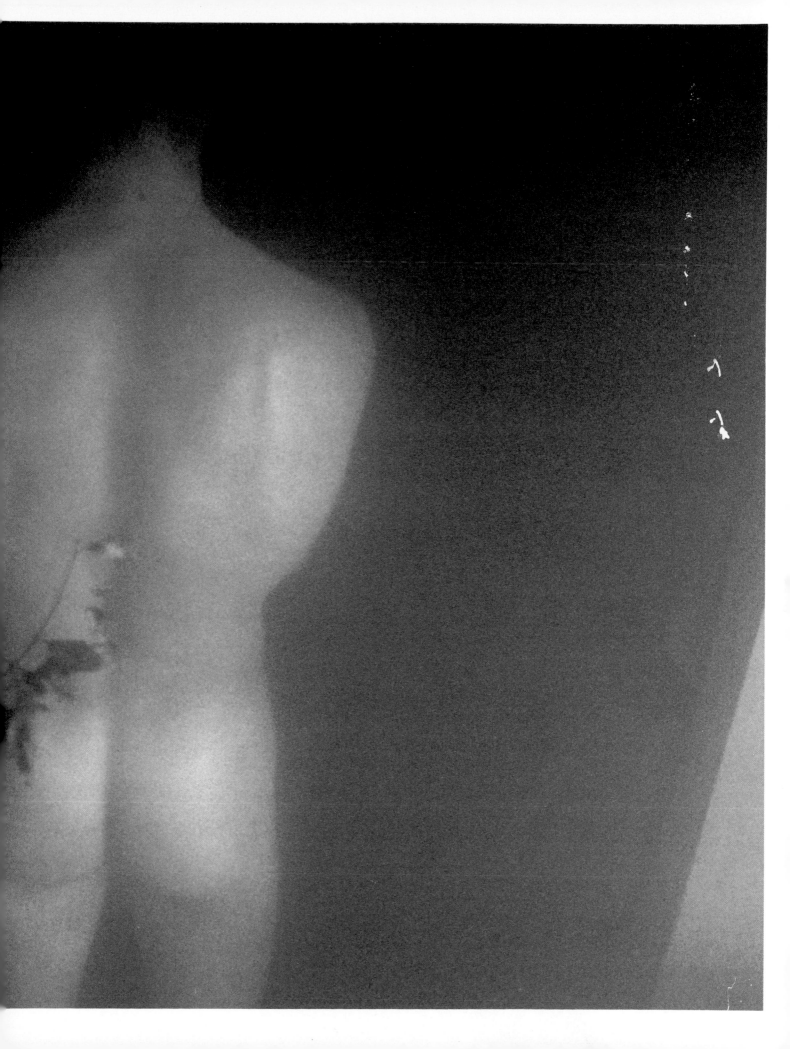

children. This salary figure is somewhat deceiving because Soviets only pay a small fraction of their salaries for rent, and health care and education are free. She likes her job. "Tomorrow I might be doing squirrels, or mink, or foxes," she says.

Nelya Chernysh inspects 2,000 minks a day. She's almost fifty years old and has worked at the factory thirty-one years. She doesn't have a mink coat herself "because they are too expensive. I have a fabric coat with mink trim."

Mink are raised mostly on farms and live six months. They are born in May, kept in cages, and fed fish porridge and liver. In November they are given an injection in their rear ends, and in a few seconds they are finished. "After all," Nelya Chernysh says, "they were raised for this purpose."

IRKUTSK, March 7

Irkutsk had a warm spell two weeks ago and all the snow has melted, leaving only patches of black ice on the street. A radio report that Reagan has been asked to resign in the wake of the Iran arms-for-hostages deal brings happiness to a carload of Soviets. The most outspoken, Victor Zemin, says Reagan must resign immediately. Zemin is also one of the most outspoken critics to a paper mill that was built on Lake Baikal. "It wounded the lake. They should be selling bottled water from that lake instead. It's the deepest freshwater lake in the world." Zemin also criticized some scientists who "were told what to say" in defense of the mill. Is he afraid to speak out? "What can they do to me?" he said. "I'm already in Siberia."

"The Arctic Ocean is 1,000 kilometers [620 miles] up there," he says pointing north. "We are 1,500 kilometers [930 miles] from Peking, 400 [248 miles] from Mongolia, and 5,500 [3,410 miles] from the Bering Strait near Alaska. So now we are standing in the middle of the earth."

He remembers the war days when the Trans-Siberian Railway carried a load of Nazi helmets toward a factory for melting. "I walked on top of them. I was only twelve, but I felt so proud."

Zemin is restoring a 1667 Russian village on the banks of the Angara River. There is a wooden tower with a house built on top of it. The floor of the house is not connected to the walls of the house. There is a several inch gap of open air. Shoddy construction? "No," says

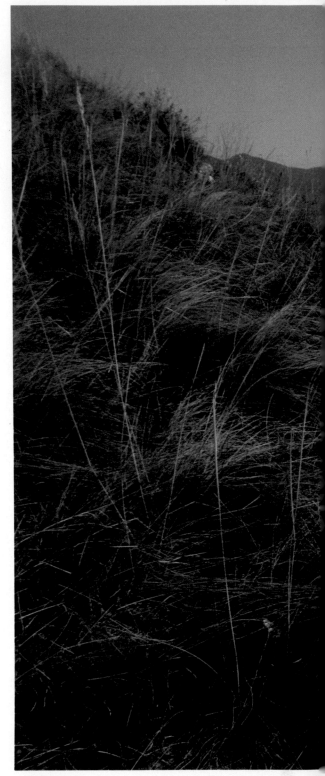

Lake Baikal

The Whisper of Stars

Zemin. "This was the last defense against attack: pour scalding water on the invaders as they climb up the stairs."

He takes us to his own home by the river. The house is filled with books; a homemade sauna sports a hand-lettered sign that reads, "If you are still in bad spirits after this steam bath, then nothing else will help."

Sit on a hillside on Lake Baikal and listen to the wind, arriving like a wave, an invisible airship, moving in stereo. Baikal, the deepest lake in the world and more than twenty-five million years old, groans as the turquoise blue ice shifts.

The great Russian writer Chekhov wrote in a letter to his sister Maria in 1890 that Baikal had "breathtakingly beautiful banks, mountains and more mountains, thickly covered with forest. As I walked ahead I felt brimming with health, words fail me to express the wonderful feeling I had."

The lake is in the shape of a wide arc, is larger than Belgium, and contains as much water as the Baltic Sea. It would take all the rivers of the world a year to fill the lake. Only the Angara flows in, although 336 rivers flow out of it. The only freshwater seals in the world reside here. The lake produces 10,000 tons of fish annually. One odd fish is the golomyanka, which lives in the darkest depths of Baikal, consists of a backbone surrounded by fat. When it is brought to the surface, it bursts like a balloon.

Edik Kovyazin, age twenty-four, looks like a cross between Larry Bird and Illya from the TV show "Man from U.N.C.L.E." He's a hunter "from birth," and he sits near the fire sipping tea and telling stories.

"It was the beginning of January, and I was hunting with my dog, Little Child. He found a wildcat that had killed a small deer on the slope of a mountain. It was burying the deer for later. The wildcat climbed up a tree, and Little Child was barking at him when I got there. My heart was pounding. I shot the wildcat. One shot between the eyes with a 28 mm shell. The cat fell. No movement. I came close and touched the body with my rifle. No movement. The dog tried to bite the wildcat. I stopped him and then touched the wildcat with the end of my shoe. Nothing. I turned my back and walked away. Little Child started barking again, and I turned around. The cat was on its feet and moving toward me. It had one eye blinded by dripping blood and was only two meters away."

Edik dips a sugar cube partially into the glass and watches the brown tea work its way toward his fingers. "I

Lake Baikal: Edik Kovyazin

The Whisper of Stars

had no time to be afraid. I shot again and killed it." He bites the sugar cube and savors the sweetness. "I sold the skin for 135 rubles and lived on wildcat steaks for weeks."

The night is frigid, and you can see the faint glow of a village on the other side of Baikal. To put the length of Baikal into perspective, it's roughly equivalent to the distance between the Bunker Hill Monument in Boston and the Washington Monument in Washington, D.C.

Horses come by the shore to graze under the half moon, their hairy manes looking like monsters rising out of the ice.

Edik, who lives here alone, confesses he would like a woman, but in winter there are none. He says it would be better with three people because he's heard stories about how two people get cabin fever and one shoots the other. Not exactly the bedtime story I want to hear.

Siberian hospitality dictates that I am given the bed nearest the log cabin's fireplace. Still, one must sleep with clothes on and try not to move. Moving means hitting another cold spot. Every couple of hours someone must get up, go outside, and get more firewood. At one point I hear a Shhhhh that might be the whisper of stars, but it is only the horses hooves scraping icy grass. Kudrya snores like the great Siberian bear whose tracks Edik has seen in the mountains.

The next day, Edik, Kudrya, and I climb steep mountains to look for spotted deer. Edik zooms up the mountains like an eagle, stopping at the first level to show a memorial in honor of a man drowned at sea. Kudrya suggests a picture as a stalling tactic to catch his breath. At the second level, a huffing and puffing Kudrya suggests we stop again and take pictures. Edik is on to something, so he and I don't stop. It is the last we see of Kudrya all day. We spot deer, but they seem to have KGB instincts. They know where we are every step of the way. Edik points to my Mt. Everest expedition Gore-Tex coat and frowns. Unlike fur, the Gore-Tex is too noisy. It's as appropriate as a Hawaiian shirt at Lenin's tomb.

At one point I ask Edik for his rifle. How would the great Hemingway have handled this? Papa Bear would have slugged down a shot of grappa and then fired a single shot for a bullseye. I ignore the deer in the distance and timidly aim for a chunk of Baikal's blue ice. When I fire, I'm taken aback as the wood grain of the rifle's barrel scrapes the whiskers on my face like sandpaper. Edik takes off his gloves, aims with my camera, and squeezes the trigger. He has trouble focusing, and his fingers on the metal are quickly pained with cold. We swap shooting tools again, this time with a new respect for each other and the smiles of friendship.

We return by a different route and are so sweaty from the hiking that steam rises off our bodies as we warm ourselves by the fireplace. Now we are communicating by charades and giggling like schoolboys. Kudrya returns later. He has dutifully waited for us to return via the same route and has the stern look of the schoolmaster betrayed.

Later, Edik punches a hole in Baikal, grabs a couple of pails, and makes a roaring fire; and we have a steam bath. As is the custom, birch branches are dipped in hot water, and we take turns beating each other with them. Then we run out into the minus 13 degree F tundra. The Siberian custom is that if you do this three times you will awake the next day a newborn baby.

As a peace gesture I offer Arkady a chance to beat me with the birch leaves. He is delighted.

In Irkutsk newborn babies are presented to their parents gift wrapped with a bow—pink for girls, blue for boys—and a flower. When they leave the hospital, the parents merely sign a receipt at the door, and then their baby finds out quickly that it's a cold, but not necessarily cruel, world outside the womb.

The saying in New England is that if you don't like the weather, wait a minute. In Siberia it is more likely to be: If you don't like the weather—too bad, comrade. Chief doctor at the Irkutsk clinic, Alekzandr Ryabtosovski, says that "It is not a firm rule, but those natives reaching the age of fifty are advised not to leave Siberia. They will not adapt well to the warmer Black Sea areas."

We go to the state-run Beriozka stores, which stock tourist items such as lacquered boxes, dolls, and fur hats. They also have such goodies as canned hams, imported wines and liquors, American cigarettes, and imported chocolates—goods that are not available to the usual Soviet citizen. They accept credit cards and foreign currency—Soviet citizens are allowed neither—and are set up to bring much-needed foreign dollars into Communist Party coffers.

Some of the elite abuse their privileges and reportedly buy here.

Kudrya, in keeping with Gorbachev's anti-alcohol reforms, says it is "not necessary" to buy any alcohol for our upcoming Trans-Siberian Railway journey even though the train is now dry. He tells me we are to share a small berth. When I insist on buying something, he suggests "perhaps a beer or two." I buy a six-pack of Tuborg, two bottles of Golden Ring vodka, and a bottle of Courvoisier.

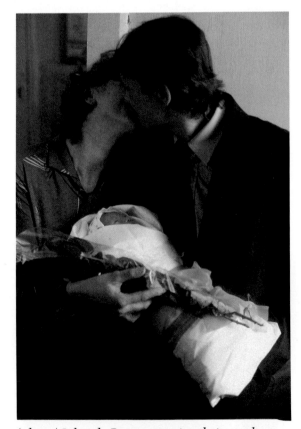

(above) Irkutsk: Parents receive their newborn baby gift-wrapped and decorated with a rose.
(opposite) Irkutsk: A nurse holds newborn twins.

The Whisper of Stars

I know of one foreigner who wanted to reward a Soviet friend who had a new baby and was struggling to make ends meet. He took him into the Beriozka shop and asked him what he would like. The Soviet man walked out of the store. The foreigner followed. "What's wrong?" he asked. "Look, I'm on an expense account. Get what you need."

His Soviet friend refused. "Someone might see me," he said. "I could get in trouble." The foreigner said he would do the shopping and his friend could wait outside in the hallway. "Someone might see and report me," he said.

They devised a plan. The foreigner bought a canned ham, a bottle of wine, some candy bars, and a pair of earrings, then walked out of the store and up some stairs. At the first landing his friend was walking down the stairs, and he handed off the package like a quarterback tucking the ball into his fullback's belly.

The Beriozka shop we are in has magazines and books. Seeing Woody Allen on the cover of a Soviet film magazine reminds me that we could use a laugh. I request a visit to the circus.

At the circus a strapping man, a solid Siberian woman, and an older man do a high-wire balancing act. Something goes wrong and they fall, but attached to safety wires they glide Peter Pan style back to earth. The audience gives them the biggest hand of the day. The performers, all native Siberians, get back on the wire and do it again, even though one of the men has suffered friction burns on his hands and is in pain. This time they succeed and are met with even louder rhythmic applause.

Watching the interaction between the parents and their children, I begin to suspect that the families here are stronger than in the West. Earlier I had watched a man giving his small son a push as he went sledding, over and over for a solid hour. I watched as a grandmother helped a granddaughter up over an icy pile of snow on the side of the road. The kid slipped and pulled her grandmother down. The two of them slid into the street, still holding hands, giggling like sisters.

Here in Siberia, there's less to fight over, to strive for, to be rewarded with. It is virtually impossible to fire Soviet workers, no matter how bad their job performances are. There are fewer material goodies to claw over. As Chekhov once wrote, it's like going to an empty well with a broken bucket.

The farther east of Red Square you go, the more relaxed and informal life gets.

Yatutsk: Rosy-cheeked children

We head for the Irkutsk train station early because the eastbound Trans-Siberian Railway train is almost always on schedule.

In 1891, the Czar sent a message to his son Nicholas, who had just arrived in the far-eastern port of Vladivostok. "I desire you lay the first stone at Vladivostok." Nicholas reportedly filled a wheelbarrow with his own hands and placed the first stone for the Great Siberian Railway. It was completed twenty-five years later and is the longest railway in the world. Irkutsk is 3,200 miles from Moscow and 2,600 from Vladivostok, on the Sea of Japan. The 5,810 miles from Moscow to Vladivostok takes seven days. The train ride cuts through six time zones and covers nearly 100 degrees in longitude. Even more amazing, this train runs on time.

As we embark on our two-and-a-half-day ride east to Khabarovsk, about thirty miles from the Chinese border, the Trans-Siberian Railway station has an electrical blackout, and shadowy figures head for beams of light spilling from the cars.

On board the *Rossiya*, or Russian, is a group of foreigners heading east toward Japan. They include a Brit heading for a motorcycle race in Japan, a West German who quit his job and is Japan bound to research tofu restaurants, and a Japanese mother and daughter returning from their second visit to Lake Baikal.

As we board the train, I snap a picture, and the conductress, Maria, sticks her tongue out in jest. For the record, photographing, filming, and sketching are forbidden at railway junctions; in tunnels, industrial areas, scientific research centers, laboratories, electricity works, radio stations, telegraph and telephone installations, military supply depots and installations, ports, and hydroelectric power stations; on road and rail bridges and signal masts; and on board planes.

On this Siberian journey only a half dozen people actually objected to any photography. But without Kudrya's help to placate those upset, I could easily have been spending a lot more time in Siberia than I had planned.

Conducters Maria and her husband, Victor, board this train in Moscow. They get off two weeks later, in Moscow. Maria works 8:00 P.M.—8:00 A.M. and Victor, 8:00 A.M.—8:00 P.M. When they get to Moscow, they have two weeks off. Maria confides that, when home, she adapts herself to a day schedule so they can have the luxury of sleeping together at night.

In the dining car there are no meat and fish left on the menu, but plenty of caviar. The waitress uses an abacus

Irkutsk: In from the Caucasus to sell apricots at the local market

The Whisper of Stars

(left) Irkutsk: Backstage at the circus
(above) A mishap sends a performer down the safety wire.
(top) The audience enjoys the circus.

Trans-Siberian Railway: Mother and child

The Whisper of Stars

for totalling up the bill, and she writes the total on the tablecloth. In another corner a waitress is cutting napkins in quarters so they will last longer. Only the foreigners seem to be using the dining car. In "hard class" they have picnics instead. Huge brown bags with grease stains contain everything from kashas to candy, fruits and fish, meats, and mountains of baked breads. To walk through the tourist class is a Peeping Tom's paradise. Some people simply never bother to get out of pajamas. Some seem to have moved whole restaurants—pots and pans and food—into the tiny rooms. Walk between cars and experience the cancer clinic. Smokers battle frostbite while sucking on Cuban cigars and Bulgarian cigarettes.

ABOARD THE TRANS-SIBERIAN RAILWAY, March 10

There's frost on the window, and Victor brews good glasses of Indian coffee served in metal holders depicting a great Soviet event—in this case, Sputnik. Outside, the terrain looks like Vermont, minus the condos and health-food shops. A man sits on the river ice with no pole, just his fishing line in his gloved hands, his fur hat flaps down over his ears. When the train stops, a small portly woman emerges from the shadows bundled in greasy clothes and a Day-Glo orange vest so that she can be seen on the tracks. She wears no gloves, and her hands are gnarled and red. She grunts as she shovels coal into one of the cars. I try to take her picture, and she starts immediately and passionately advocating a form of Gorbachev's new policy of *perestroika* (restructure). Specifically, she wants to *perestroika* my nose.

Safely inside the train, I find the berths are very comfortable. Each is six feet long and about four feet wide. Each compartment has three mirrors, reading lamps above the beds, Indian-style rugs, 16" x 20" tables, storage under the beds, and, above the door, two coat hangers and a towel per person. Soft, or first, class contains two beds per compartment; hard class has four beds. Flush the toilet in the spanking clean bathrooms and steam rises. If you are looking for a shower, pray for rain or get invited into the conductor's personal bathroom.

The train reaches a plateau, and there is an old cemetery with a humble rusted iron fence around it. Perhaps this is where a few of the more than 30,000 men

Trans-Siberian Railway:
Victor the conductor

who built this railroad are laid to rest. Some of those men were convicts, given one year off their sentences for eight months' work on the railroad. The cemetery commands a peaceful view of a bend in the river and a small village below.

Arkady picks up a copy of *New Time*, a Soviet weekly of world affairs, and proudly translates it. Here in full is an article as it appeared in the March 14, 1987, edition.

In the United States last year the American journalist Seymour M. Hersh published a book entitled *The Target Is Destroyed, What Really Happened to Flight 007 and What America Knew About It*. In the book he presents hitherto unknown evidence relating to the provocative flight of the South Korean airliner.

The first piece of evidence goes back to the pre-flight period and shows that such operations had been conceived long before. "In the spring of 1983, Ronald Reagan," Hersh writes, "after many months of relative restraint, condemned the Soviets as an 'evil empire' and challenged the legitimacy of the Soviet government. Thousands of miles away from the White House press corps and the presidential talk of 'evil empire,' the United States Pacific Fleet was beginning its largest maneuvers since World War Two in the North Pacific. During the three-week exercise, Navy warplanes from the aircraft carriers *Midway* and *Enterprise* directly overflew Soviet military installations on the Kuril Islands just north of Japan.

"American warships were authorized by the President late in March to operate and exercise closer to Soviet borders than ever before. In all, 23,000 American military men took part."

Seymour Hersh's next piece of evidence refers to the autumn of 1983, the first few days after the South Korean plane had been shot down over Soviet territory in the pursuit of its espionage mission. He writes:

"Some senior Air Force and Navy officers in the Pacific. . .'got emotional,' as one officer recalled, and began formulating actions for retaliation against the Soviet Union, actions 'that could have started World War Three.' The officer, who was stationed in the Pacific, told of being approached by an Air Force general and asked to forward an essentially fraudulent intelligence report to the Pentagon that was designed to justify acts of provocation against the Soviet Union."

"That's bullshit," I said, doing my little part to teach Kudrya American slang. "I will get this book and show you the quotes," he said. "I know the quotes are in there, but I read that book and that's not even what the

Trans-Siberian Railway: Soviets dine in their berths, picnic style.

book's about. Let's talk about the little kids who were on that flight." All I hear is the rumble of tracks.

We are products of two different cultures, both filled with home-brewed propaganda. In the United States, President Reagan calls the Soviet Union an "evil empire." Kids grow up watching movies like *Rambo: First Blood Part II*, in which the American hero is apparently shot down by a laughing Soviet pilot while trying to retrieve POWs in Vietnam.

In the U.S.S.R. the Soviet government-controlled media image is of an America where homeless people roam the streets, blacks are treated inhumanely, and big American companies get rich by selling war weapons.

Upon my return home I sent the *Moscow News* article to Hersh at the *New York Times* Washington bureau. In a telephone interview, he called the article "a bizarre and sinister extrapolation. But so what? That's standard fare over there."

Back on the train I put on the Walkman a tape by the great revolutionary leader John Lennon. The Soviet policy on rock and roll was reflected in a Novosti question-and-answer book that Kudrya urged me to buy. "The worship of pop music may lead to a real spiritual bankruptcy and moral degradation," the book said. "We will never tire of fighting this evil."

Turning up the volume, I write the lyrics to the song in my notebook. "I've had enough of reading things by neurotic, psychotic, pigheaded politicians. All I want is the truth, just give me some truth."

"Arkady?" I said.

"Yes."

" 'All I want is the truth. Just give me some truth.' Lennon said that."

"Of course. I know Lenin said that."

"Good night, Arkady."

"Good night."

ABOARD THE TRANS-SIBERIAN RAILWAY, March 11

The Trans-Siberian runs on Moscow time because the Soviet Union has eleven time zones. Arkady passes most of his day beating an Armenian named Arthur at chess.

Arthur lives near the Amur River in Siberia. He was born in Armenia and is on his way back to Siberia from a tearful reunion with his brothers and sisters. When he was a teenager in the Red Army he was stationed in Siberia. He fell in love, with both the land and a woman, and stayed.

Trans-Siberian Railway

As a bottle of Golden Ring vodka dries up, he tells us how years ago the Chinese and Russians continually had border clashes. "The Damansky Islands lie in the Ussuri River between Russia and China. In 1968 the Soviets said it was theirs, China said it was theirs. When forty of our soldiers were killed, we blew up the island. It's not there anymore."

Arthur, a big strong man with white hair and hairy arms, wants his picture taken with the Polaroid. He gets the print and excuses himself; when he returns, his head is high and his chest is puffed out proudly. He presents a big red Armenian apple, a present indeed in a land where fruit is usually canned or bottled. Arkady brings some bread, smoked fish, and sprats, which taste like canned smoked sardines.

Arkady and Norbert, the German man en route to the tofu paradise of Japan, discuss World War Two. Arkady says that Stalin wasn't totally to blame for the purges. It was the people under him. Norbert said that people blame him for Hitler, and he wasn't even born.

Victor and Maria open up an empty compartment and put out vanilla wafers, oranges, and a bottle of Armenian cognac. They tell us how they met on this very train, fifteen years ago.

"I was in car 7 and Maria was in car 14 or 15. Somewhere in Siberia we passed in the hallway and neither of us looked out the window. I invited Maria for some tea."

"And some wine," Maria said, smiling broadly so you could see the space between her teeth.

"One week later we were married," he said.

They ask me to sign their logbook, and I write that Gorbachev and Reagan should be forced to share a compartment on the Trans-Siberian Railway.

All foreigners must leave the Trans-Siberian Railway at Khabarovsk, west of Vladivostok. Vladivostok is a heavily militarized city on the Pacific Ocean and closed to foreigners.

The Intourist cabdriver who pulls his cab up on the platform to meet the train refuses a tip, asking instead for American cigarettes. The sign in his cab reads, "Let there be peace to the whole of humanity around the world." There is less snow but more soldiers here than at any other stop. We are sixty kilometers from the Chinese border.

The Intourist brochure photos of the various Soviet cities have been predictably boring. Moscow is a snapshot of Red Square. Novosibirsk has Lenin and the five statues. Irkutsk, a modern hotel. But in Khabarovsk it's different. The photo shows a blonde-haired woman, in a

Naikhan: Siberian child

(above) Naikhan: Hunter
(left) Khabarovsh: Ban the bomb.
(overleaf) Troitskoye: Typical Siberia, warm and orangey on the inside,
icy and blue on the outside. Only the legs of a woman who stopped briefly
during this time exposure are registered on film.

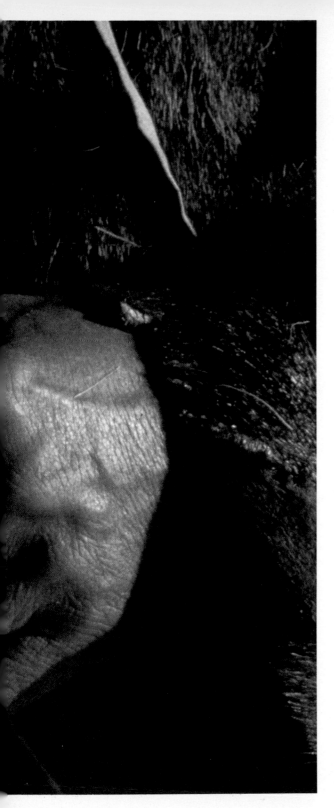

mid-calf dress, facing a statue. The summer breeze has blown the dress to one side so you can see a long length of leg. The brochure says things are going up here. "More and more nine, eleven, and fourteen-storied houses appear." The Soviets are proud of this because most of the housing built during Khrushchev's regime is five-story concrete. "Khrushchev housing" is ugly and unpopular with residents. People are so desperate to leave these aging buildings that they are willing to lose some of their existing living space to do it. For example, if you had a four-room "Khrushchev flat," you would get only a three-room new apartment.

Khabarovsk was named after the seventeenth-century explorer E. P. Khabarov and was built on a series of seven hills. It lies at the intersection of the Ussuri and the Amur valleys in a key strategic location commanding the road to Chinese Manchuria. Most people among the 500,000 citizens look Asiatic. Moscow is eight hours away by air, seven days away by train.

In 1918 the American cruiser *Brooklyn* anchored in the Siberian port of Vladivostok. American troops, ordered in by the Wilson Administration, remained in the area of Khabarovsk for two years. Recently, the Soviet answer to the "Amerika" TV show was to release a series of articles about American atrocities during that period.

One article, entitled "American Intervention in Civil War: Sinister Memories," claims:

> The Americans broke into the house of Vasily Nasonov, a retired miner, and attacked Liza, his granddaughter. Trying to protect her, the old man was knocked down with a rifle butt. He stood up and spat into a rapist's face. The soldiers kicked him and beat him with their rifle butts until he was unconscious and dragged him to their headquarters.
>
> Another group of soldiers brought the villager Kuzma Privalov, who had also attempted to protect a young woman relative. Both men were hanged.
>
> Nikolai Myasnikov, a guerilla, was taken prisoner in the battle of Sviyagino village, March 1919. Andrei Yatsenko, his comrade in arms, later testified that Myasnikov had been cruelly tortured as Americans tried to make him reveal guerilla stationing, which he did not know. They cut off his ears and nose, and then his hands and feet. The man was chopped to pieces alive.

The article is written by Eugene I. Bugayenko, chief editor for Novosti's Far East bureau. A short man with a firm handshake, he will accompany Kudrya and me in the Khabarovsk area. His initial greeting: "I hope you are in the mood to do good work and not take pictures of garbage."

The Whisper of Stars

Troitskoye: A Siberian woman balances pails of water drawn from a community well as she walks to her home.

Later the Soviet newspaper *Komsomol* would display a photo of a man digging into a garbage can in Great Britain. The caption said such rummaging is a result of Thatcher's government policies. It just so happened she would be meeting with Gorbachev the next week.

Bugayenko has taken the initiative to hire a helicopter to take us to see hunters in the taiga. The cost to me will be $4,000 but will place us within close proximity of his favorite fishing spot. We will need a helicopter later to reach some remote villages. But not now. I tell him to cancel the trip. "I called the airport, and they were very angry until I told them American capitalism is in crisis. It calmed them down," he told me.

A cruise down Karl Marx Street reveals only one line of people. It is for *moroshoyne*, or ice cream, which in Siberia is creamy and delicious.

That evening, under cover of darkness, we head north out of town for Troitskoye.

"No American or non-Communist person has ever set foot there," Bugayenko says.

"We are taking two cabs. The road is bad. The last time I went there a rock kicked up from a lumber truck and smashed my windshield. Then my axle broke and I sat there for ten hours until somebody came along."

"Troikskoye is a Nannai village, population 6,000. They used to have their own state in the eighth to twelfth centuries in the Khabarovsk region. But the Mongolians attacked and almost wiped them out. On the eve of the Revolution they were on the brink of death.

"The Nannai, who were hunters and fishermen, were in the beginning slow to learn new techniques. Once they were taught how to plant potatoes. They waited one, two, three days, no potatoes—so they dug them up and ate the bulbs."

The road has turned from hardtop to dirt to gravel pit. A fire burns brightly by the side of the road. It is made by a log-truck driver whose truck has broken down.

We arrive in the village near midnight and are met by Ivan, a local Communist Party secretary. He wears a gray polyester suit and a blue shirt and brown tie. Nannai people look like a combination of Indian and Eskimo.

In the hotel lobby four people stare at me as if I had just arrived from Mars.

TROITSKOYE, March 13

At 6:00 A.M. there is a fresh coat of snow on Troitskoye, a village of log houses about eight streets wide and two

(left) Naikhan: Students jam a local classroom to see something they've never seen before in person — an American.
(above) Troitskoye: At dawn, a man uses a broom to brush away light snow.

Troitskoye: Nannai folk dance

  *The Whisper of Stars*

miles long. A morning walk alone is a reward for sleeping in the same room with the great Siberian snoring bear.

Villagers grab buckets and poles and head for the numerous wells for water. Three truck drivers are perched under their hoods trying to start their rigs in the minus 13 degree F chill.

The walk ends as Arkady and Eugene (pronounced Ivgainey) inform me we have a meeting at the local soviet, or town hall. Arkady suggests a shave. The borrowed blade feels like it was used in the 1917 Revolution. There is no shaving cream, no hot water, and no toilet paper. But who's complaining? I've discovered a good use for *Pravda*.

The first question the local soviet group has is about Kool-Aid. They want to know how many Americans drank it at Jim Jones's commune in Guyana.

The next question is, "What do you think of the TV series 'Amerika?' " This is by far the single most frequently asked question in Siberia, and articles about it dominate the Soviet press. Sometimes I answer we have lots of bad TV shows in America and "Amerika" is just one of many. Sometimes I answer that I fell asleep in part one and never tuned in again. Sometimes I answer that what the Soviet press doesn't report is that "Amerika" was universally reviewed in the media as garbage. Sometimes I answer that I only tuned in to see Mariel Hemingway, and that was before I found out she had breast implants and I'm depressed and don't want to talk about it anymore.

Across the street at the Palace of Culture, an American movie, *A Man From A Star*, is playing. In Troitskoye you can buy only one bottle of vodka once a month, a law enacted by the local soviet. Being Nannai has some privileges, too, however. They have their own language and textbooks, music school for all is free (instead of 23 rubles a month), hunting licenses are free, and 88 pounds of salmon are given to each family in September.

Before Nannai old-timers go fishing, they throw out rice and bread on the water "to please the spirits." When they get married they have part of the ceremony on the river, the groom chasing the bride in a kayak. When they die they are buried in their winter clothes and winter hats. The men are buried with their guns and knives, the women with their needles and yarn. "The old customs are dying with the old people," says Ivan.

In the nearby village of Naikhan, just nineteen miles down the frozen Cherochin River, the local schoolchildren jam into a classroom to practice the English they've been learning since the fourth grade. It is a friendly audience. A standing ovation is mine just for saying "drastwizia," or hello in Russian. Another when a Polaroid camera spits out an instant picture.

On the wall are quilts, letters, and photos from an elementary school in Drain, Oregon. "It is a mystery to us," one student explains. "One day it just arrived."

It still is a mystery. A school in Drain, Oregon, said the package was mailed two years previously to another village 200 miles away. The students are preparing a similar package to send to Drain. I chose a letter at random to be translated from Russian to English:

Dear friend,

I am a schoolgirl of the seventh form (grade). I live in the Far East of the U.S.S.R., in the village Naikhan of the Khabarovsk region.

I am happy because I was born in the Soviet Union. Our country lives in peace and the sky over us shines brighter and brighter.

Our village is very beautiful, the nature around us is very rich. Every summer our family goes fishing. There are a lot of fish at our place. And in the forest there are a lot of mushrooms. Every fall our father brings from the forest cedar nuts.

I study quite well. I like skiing and playing basketball. My favorite subject in school is chemistry.

I, as all children of the Soviet Union, want to live in peace and we fight for peace.

We organize in our school a special fair of solidarity. We sell goods and toys we make ourselves and send money to the Soviet peace fund. We also organize a competition for best posters devoted to peace.

I dream about the day when all wars will be eliminated from our life and all people will learn and work.

It will be a happy life for everyone on the earth.

Your friend, Tanya Glushakova.

The students of Naikhan are filled with questions. They want to know how much we pay for college? What boys and girls in America do for fun? What are we doing to remember Samantha Smith in America? What kind of music do we like? Where do we go on vacation? They present me with a Samantha Smith peace pin, a native Nannai doll, two pairs of slippers, and a Nannai textbook.

I present them with the treasures of capitalism: eight packs of tutti-frutti gum, a Minnie Mouse Disneyland pin, and several Polaroid pictures of the class to put in the massive peace package they are sending to Drain. Bruce Springsteen's "Born in the USA" tape is given to a blonde teenager wearing a thin tie who says he loves rock and roll. Judging from his initial reaction, however, The Boss is just another proletariat stiff.

Troitskoye: A young boy checks the house before a local show.

(above) Troitskoye: Nannai children and frozen laundry (right)

Cherochin Riber: A football field's worth of net yields plenty of bounty. (opposite) A man keeps his puppy bundled in his fur coat.

I ask them if they worry about a nuclear war? Unanimously, yes. With the United States? Another yes. One young girl wants all nuclear armaments destroyed; another girl worries that there are more girls than boys and "it is a problem."

I tell them that the people in America don't want a nuclear war. I ask them if the Russian kids fight with the Nannai kids? They laugh. They want autographs on postcards and scraps of paper, and they line the halls to shake hands.

The students in their black-and-white uniforms follow us outside and wave until we are out of sight and back on the river.

Our entourage has grown to eight men counting drivers, local Soviet leaders, journalists from Novosti, and a local newspaper reporter. The lead car cruises over an ice fisherman's hole in the frozen river and the rear tire plops in.

The men surround the car to lift it and are too proud to let a guest help.

Farther down river, eight Nannai fishermen have drilled four holes in the ice and spread enough net to cover a football field. One of them saw Americans in 1961 when he was on a fishing vessel near San Francisco. The Americans came close in motorboats to wave and take pictures. The bounty is good, and the fish go into a deep freeze in minutes. Then they are scaled and cut in thin strips called *stroganina* and served frozen with wasabi, soy sauce, and chopped onions. It is delicious.

At the local fish cooperative they claim to handle 400,000 tons of salmon. There are some pamphlets on a billboard, and I pick one. To my surprise it is a handwritten pledge of resolutions. "I pledge to work 110% for the Lenin School of Community Studies. To compete with Valentina Patermina in productivity. To struggle for the leader of the Communist Party."

The next one is completely different. "I pledge to . . . treat fish in a good way . . . not to waste anything . . . and to participate in the public life of the farm."

Those who meet their obligations get bonuses such as radios and televisions. I am given a huge smoked salmon and told to bring it to America.

The whirlwind schedule includes a visit to a Nannai folk-dance performance that is colorful, proud, and festive. And a visit to a local woman doctor. Women doctors make up 70 percent of all doctors in the Soviet Union. This doctor's husband complains that his wife is always busy making house calls. Now she is preparing dinner. Although our schedule always calls for three

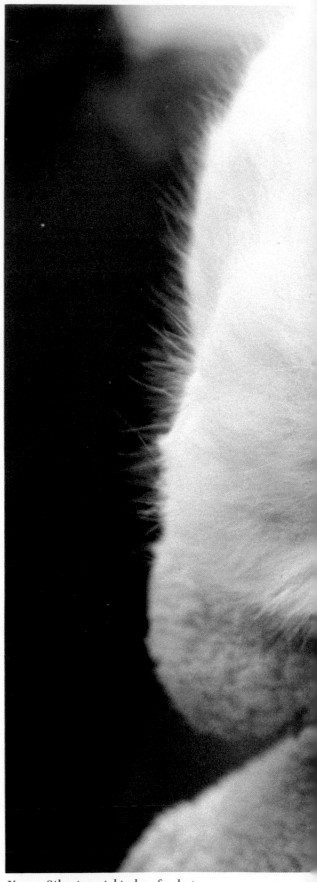

Young Siberian girl in her fur hat

The Whisper of Stars

(above) Khabarovsk: Siberian food — grains, carrots, and cabbage
(right) Pork in Novosibirsk

The Whisper of Stars

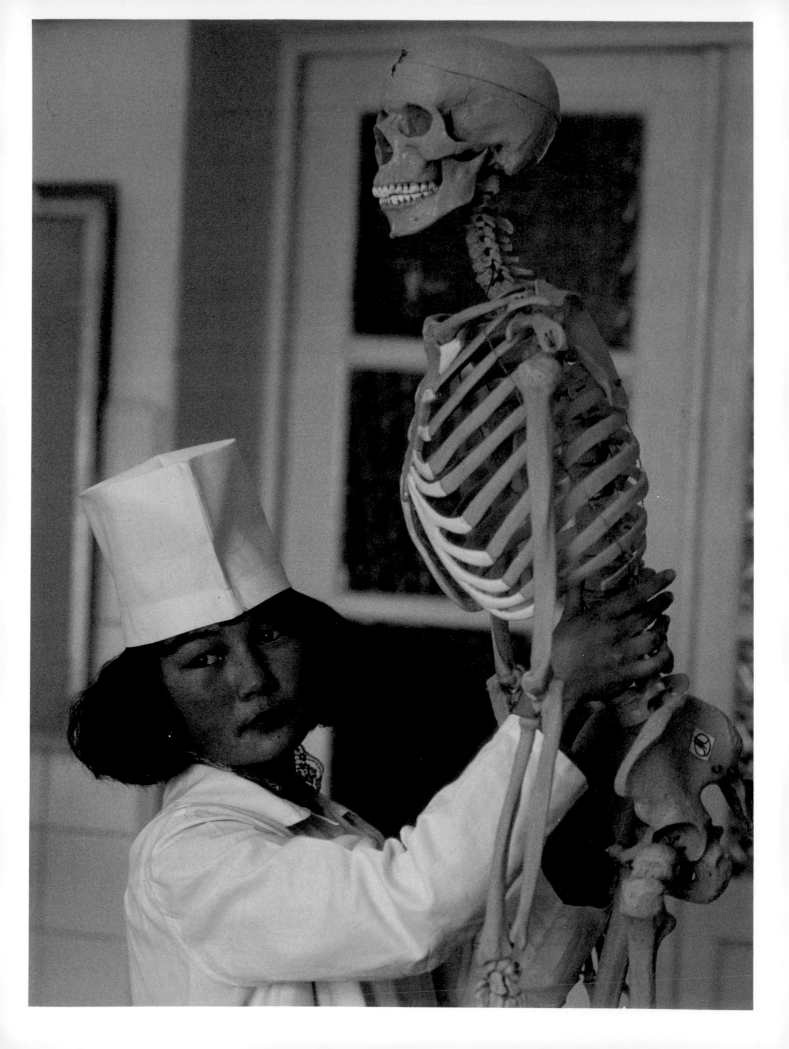

meals a day in hotels and restaurants, I have learned to eat sparingly.

Wherever we go there are elaborate spreads specially prepared for us. The hosts are always insulted if we do not eat, even if we have just eaten. In this home they don't speak English but have baked an apricot cake with the words "Good evening" on it. Above the sink in the bathroom, is a tub, which they have filled with hot water from the kettle in the kitchen. Siberian hospitality.

The last stop is the local soviet, where I am presented a book with a specially printed page with my name in Russian, commemorating the visit of the first American, and a wish for peace.

It is now almost midnight, and I ask if we can stay another night. Nyet. The mystique of Siberia. We must drive at night back through the gravel-pit roads to arrive at Khabarovsk at 4:00 A.M.

The great Siberian bear snores in the front seat, and I give the upholstery an occasional kick when I can make it seem like a bump in the road.

KHABAROVSK, March 14

In an English language lab at a local medical school, students are asked if they know that AIDS has started spreading to the heterosexual community. They don't know that. Soviets are not preoccupied with AIDS. Soviet authorities report only thirty-two AIDS cases. According to *Soviet Life*, "among these are thirty foreign students and trainees. After supportive treatment, twenty-eight of the infected individuals have returned home. Unfortunately, two of the foreigners died in the hospital. The country's best doctors are still battling for the two Soviet patients' lives."

Nuclear war, however, is an entirely different matter.

One woman, Anzhela Karikmasova, says that she has nightmares about a nuclear blast. "There is this terrible huge dark blast," she says, as a skeleton hangs limply nearby. "The sight and sound are scary, and I start crying and my friend starts crying. We start hugging and kissing each other good-bye."

That evening Eugene, Arkady, and I go for a picnic in the beautiful taiga. We are within thirty miles of China when the car gets stuck in the snow. Everyone works up a sweat as we cut birch branches and lay them down in front of the tires to build a path. After liberating the car we drink vodka and eat raw, frozen fish around a huge campfire. Eugene confides that the local Soviets didn't

Khabarovsk: Medical student Anzhela Karikmosova

like a quick street photo of an old woman with a cane. I tell him that I am not doing picture postcards for Intourist brochures.

Though harsh at times, Soviet life has some good qualities we can learn from. I tell them I sincerely admire their free health care, closer knit families, earlier learning of languages, and appreciation of nature.

Eugene says he is a member of the Communist Party. He says to become one you need three recommendations from Communist Party members who have known you for more than a year. The local party meets and votes. Then you become a "candidate" for a year. Then they meet and vote again.

Are there special privileges for being in the Communist Party? Kudrya snaps his fingers, a subconscious sign that what he is about to say is important. "Nyet," he says. "Just the opposite. During World War Two, Communist Party members went to the front lines first." I wonder aloud if they don't abuse their privileges by buying goods at Beriozka shops that the average citizen can't use? There is a reply, but its meaning is overpowered by the burning sensation of a straight shot of vodka and the search for a hunk of the rich brown bread to absorb it.

The talk turns to KAL Flight 007 again. Arkady makes the point that Flight 007 is a spy plane and Eugene agrees.

"There were children on that plane, and why have a spy plane when you can see a license plate from a satellite photo?" I ask. This point never gets translated. Arkady wonders why we are escalating the threat of war with Star Wars? I ask why the Soviets never warned the world of the Chernobyl nuclear accident. The ride back is silent.

I retire to my room and then head out alone. It's Saturday night and the people whom I talk to in pidgin Russian are filled with smiles and good cheer for an American. Two women from whom I ask directions accompany me to a disco. It's 9:45 P.M., but the doors are locked.

Depressed. Return to the room alone.

Donahue on TV. More depressed.

Khabarovsk: Youngster on a ride at Farewell to Winter Festival

KHABAROVSK, March 15

Spent an hour staring out the window, finally realizing that behind one of the brick walls two blocks away are a dozen Soviet tanks. The English stations on the short-

wave radio are talking about imperialist America this and imperialist America that. No Voice of America or BBC here. Finally a station called "Super Rock" from Taipei skips in and then out.

At breakfast, Kudrya says "I like you because you are not afraid to eat the native foods." The chef serves something called *holdets*, which is beef packed in gelatin. I do not care for it because it reminds me of the open-heart surgery in Akademgordok. Because fresh fruit is scarce in Siberia, I have made a point of drinking as much juice as I can hold. Glass after glass after glass.

"This apple juice is delicious," I say, pouring another glass. "Apple?" says Kudrya with a smile and a snap of the fingers. "That's prune."

The hotel bathroom has two air hand dryers that are made in the Soviet Union but look remarkably similar to the ones in the United States.

Neither of them work.

It's 20 degrees F, but the wind chill makes today's "Farewell to Winter Festival" seem like an endurance test.

Surprisingly, thousands of people show up on the banks of the Amur River to celebrate. There are caviar, shish kebab, beef Stroganoff, and cookies. All in abundance and no lines. It is fun until I take some photographs of Red Army soldiers. "Don't photograph them," says Eugene Bugayenko. Now it is no longer fun.

There is a long parade of arm-in-arm revelers who have formed a train weaving through the crowd. At the last second I sprint past the lead merrymakers. My companions are stuck on the other side, as at a railroad crossing. Two pretty medical students who were interviewed the previous day dance down the street. They hook my arm and together we go skipping down Karl Marx Street.

At the Cafe Youth, operated by Komsomol (Communist Youth League), the age eighteen-to-thirty crowd dances to a song by Madonna. It's a slow dance with enough space between couples for two copies of *War and Peace*.

Sergei Skorimov, who looks like a yuppie insurance agent but is Deputy of Ideology, gives his views on sex. "It's not good to kiss on the first date." An unscientific poll is taken at one table about premarital sex in Siberia. The results: Two say they are for it, two say it could happen, one is against it, and one wants to know "why you are escalating the Star Wars program."

Still, baby making is a national pastime in these parts, and for good reason. After World War Two, the Soviet Union had twenty-five million more women than men.

Khabarovsk: Farewell to Winter Festival

The Whisper of Stars

Women were encouraged to have children, whether they were married or not. The fathers, by law, were relieved of financial responsibility, with the state picking up the tab. In 1957, at the peak of the program, there were more than three million unwed mothers. Today, women in Siberia who bear children get medals.

Five get you a silver medal, ten a gold. The Soviets are trying to populate mineral-rich Siberia, and medals and special privileges serve as incentives—just flash your medal and go to the front of the line.

The Cafe is open from 7:00 P.M.–10:30 P.M. Admission is one ruble, and a set menu consisting of red berry juice, salad, chicken leg with potatoes, and cake is three rubles ($4.50). The women wear long skirts or pants, and there are not enough men to dance with. The disc jockey plays the top Soviet groups, "Dynamic" and "Aquarium." Then there is a slide show about the wonders of Yugoslavia.

Now it's contest time. A slide is projected of a volleyball and a tomato side by side. Everyone is asked to write the caption. The winner will get a small prize, no one knows exactly what. Perhaps the prize is the tomato. The last fresh tomato I saw was 2,000 miles ago. But then again, in America you can't walk into a store, plunk down one ruble and buy a plastic pouch of frozen pineapple chunks stamped "Product of Vietnam."

YAKUTSK, March 16

The earth is black from 30,000 feet in the air, and there is a band of pink hugging it. On top of that is a thin band of green and then a band of blue. We are heading north toward Yakutsk. If you stood in Moscow, you would be closer to Boston than Yakutsk. For a solid three hours there have been no clouds below us and no sign of life in the Siberian night. We are talking end of the world here.

Finally, as the plane descends toward Yakutsk, a faint glow of orange brightens the blue snow. Could it be hunters curled close to a fire? Once on the ground the night becomes darker, as if the sun got out of bed, took a peek, and decided to curl up under a blanket of clouds.

Half of the Soviet Union is covered by permafrost— permanently frozen ground. Since 1943 the Soviets have built their houses on stilts sunk into the ground. Prior to that, when the top few feet thawed out in the summer, houses sank. All heating systems are above ground so as not to melt the permafrost.

"In winter we practically don't see the sun, not only because daytime is short but because of the habitation

(left) Construction workers build houses on stilts that won't sink in the brief summer thaw.

(above) Yakutsk: Permafrost covering half the Soviet Union requires that pipes be put above ground.

The Whisper of Stars

fog, which starts appearing at minus 40 degrees F and covers Yakutsk like a big hat," said one of my local escorts. Habitation fog is formed by the exhalations of both man and machine. This frozen "people mist" hovers over villages like an eerie blue funk. It causes accidents and flight cancellations.

There are extra perks for life in a freezer. Workers here get forty-two days of vacation a year. In Siberia the government awards its frequent freezers with a free round-trip air ticket to anywhere in the U.S.S.R. every other year. Double salary after only five years. Nevertheless, many people leave after a year.

"This winter it got to be 60 [minus 76 degrees F]. Last summer it got real hot—36 [plus 96 degrees F]. If you put our record high and low together you get 96 degrees [172 degrees F]. No other city in the world has this span," says my guide.

"When the temperature hits 56 [minus 68.8 degrees F] all classes up to the seventh grade are cancelled. All children are happy because they can play hockey. But it's very hard to walk fast, there's a shortage of oxygen, and it hurts to breathe."

"Last New Year's Eve it was 60 [minus 76.8 degrees F]. People celebrated anyway," he says, studying his visitor's face.

"You must watch it if you get a white spot on your skin. You must rub it with pure wool until the spot disappears. The eyes don't freeze, but we try not to cry outside. Here we get two seasons. Summer in June, July, and half of August. You must come back in summer; the mosquitoes love the blood of foreigners."

He laughs, then continues. "Then it snows. The first snow always melts, and then the leaves turn yellow. In one week winter comes."

The Hotel Lena has a decompression-chamber system to get into the lobby. You have to go through three doors to shake the cold. Triple-paned windows are taped shut. Other apartment buildings have huge cloth sacks under their windows, free freezer space. The roads are always in need of repair due to the summer thaw which has the effect of an earthquake, heaving pavement, twisting telephone poles, and sinking the old log-cabin houses. Only one type of tree, a spreading branched tamarack, can survive here. When it gets to be minus 58 degrees F and you think you hear birds chirping, head for the nut house.

Today Yakutsk is known for its gold and diamond mining. The really big diamonds are named after famous people. The last big diamond was named after Samantha Smith. The city (population 33,000 with fourteen differ-

The Whisper of Stars

Yatutsk: At the Permafrost Institute scientists study the phenomenon of permanently frozen ground.

(above) Yatutsk: College students wear white, polar fox hats made for them by their grandmothers.
(opposite) Dusk, downtown Yatutsk

ent nationalities) used to be known as a frontier town with wild drinking, parties, and brawls. The only thing people used to worry about was leaving their vodka out when the temperature hit minus 46 degrees F. Then it froze into a clear block of ice. Now you need a ticket to buy one bottle of vodka or two bottles of champagne once a month, and the price of vodka has doubled since last year. The good news is that beer sales are unlimited, the bad news is that they have no beer to sell.

"If you were drunk and fell in the street in Moscow, it's nothing," says my local escort. "Here you're dead. There is some abuse, some home brew, but many women are happy. The law makes the family stronger."

For the last week I have been searching in vain for shaving cream. Finally a store here has it—Soviet made and in a squeezeable tube. In the morning I mistake it for toothpaste.

If you want to reach out and touch someone with a frosty phone call from Siberia, get in line. A solo stop at a phone center reveals 225 souls waiting to use twenty-two phone booths, two of which were broken. Four operators look harried, and people look much sadder than the faded color slides of smiling Ukrainian dancers enlarged on the walls.

Most of our dinners on the trip have been held in private dining rooms at the hotel. This evening, while returning to the hotel, I see two young ladies with white polar-fox hats. Kudrya walks briskly up the steps and into the hotel. I photograph the ladies then present them with a Polaroid print for a present. In broken Russian I invite them to dinner. They accept, and the three of us stroll into the lobby just as Kudrya is strolling out to find me. They are students in college. Their grandmothers made them the white polar-fox hats, which sell in Moscow for $100 and in Saks Fifth Avenue for $400.

Over a dinner of fried sturgeon and champagne, Sardina says that she has thirteen brothers and sisters. I ask if her mother has the gold hero medal for having more than ten children, and she says she has never seen it. She says her mother had two husbands, though, so maybe that's why she doesn't have a medal. Maybe there is an asterisk after her name in the record book.

YAKUTSK, March 17

The woman at the Aeroflot counter stares at a small orange glowing portable heater shaped like a satellite dish. Heat is the only signal she wants to receive. We are headed north again toward the Arctic Circle.

The Aeroflot prop plane first heads to Khandyga,

Yatusk: Sunken house, pre-1943 construction

where the radar dish revolves on the roof of a log cabin. Aeroflot flight attendant Olga Kanitskaya says they stop flying when the temperature hits minus 69 degrees F. One hopes at that point that you are on the ground. The plane refuels and continues north.

In Ust' Nera, Nikolai Gabyshev, grinning so that four gold-capped teeth sparkle, asks me if I would prefer deluxe or regular accommodation at the Sunny Hotel. "Deluxe," I say, without hesitation, hoping deluxe means "with toilet seat," a luxury the last hotel didn't have. Siberian hotels where foreign tourists stay are very clean and comfortable, although somewhat small. In this part of Siberia, tourists are not allowed, and there are no Intourist hotels. After rattling through the now-standard three-door entrance, I am escorted to a four-room suite that was home to the Prince of Iran shortly before Khomeini seized power. The prince is gone, but the throne remains in the bathroom.

Ust' Nera is in the Omyakon Region, but it is the village of Omyakon where journalists want to go. The village in 1933 recorded a temperature of minus 96 degrees F, lowest in the Northern Hemisphere and lowest of any village in the world. The schedule in every town or village calls for a meeting with the local soviet leaders. It is like interviewing the mayor of Secaucus, New Jersey, when you want the mayor of New York City.

Ivan Dyakonov, chairman of the district, contends that "people in Omyakon come here [Ust' Nera] and they freeze. Omyakon is in a valley, and it's true the temperatures are colder. But Omyakon gets no wind. Here there is a wind. Here it is colder."

At a local Soviet Pioneers Center—the Soviet equivalent of our daycare centers—the kids sing patriotic songs accompanied by an accordion. The schoolkids ask, "What toys do kids have in America?" It is obvious that they have few.

I speak without thinking. "We have huge department stores filled with nothing but toys. When I was a kid, I had so many toys stored on a shelf over my bed that one night it just collapsed on me while I was sleeping." The kids looked stunned. Big department stores filled with just toys. (I am thinking of Toys "Я" Us.) I have hurt their feelings. The combination of intense cold, the month-long peppering of propaganda, and those middle-of-the-night flights has taken its toll. I am Jerks "Я" Us. I send Arkady back to the room. "Tell them I said toys are not what's important. A good imagination is far more important than any toy." The word comes back. The kids want my address so we can be pen pals.

Ust' Nera: When I approached a women's swimming class with my camera, the members devoted most of their energies to moving away from me.
(opposite) Ust' Nera: Indoor soccer
(overleaf) Omyakon: Reindeer breeder in the taiga

(above) Omyakon: Three curious schoolchildren
(opposite) Selennyakh Mountains viewed from a helicopter: So cold
and remote as to be uninhabited by man.

Let's talk cold. At 6:15 A.M. I emerge from my princely pad at the Sunny Hotel and walk through the three doors of doom into minus 49 degrees F. Breath number one: The nose hairs freeze together. Exhale: The nose hairs thaw out. Within ten minutes the fingers ache despite three layers of gloves. Silk first, then wool, then polypropylene.

The full moon's intensity is cloaked by a fog that casts a deep, dark, depressing blue over the village. The early morning lights in the log cabin look extra inviting, warm orange spilling into cold blue. Street lights go off, making the contrast more pronounced. The village is in a blue funk from four steam factories pouring blue steam into cold mountain air, just to keep it alive. Five hundred trucks bring coal from Magadan on the Sea of Okhotsk, 620 miles away. The road is icy, dark, and treacherous, and the vehicles that slide off those mountain curves look like little tombstones at the bottom of these cliffs.

The trucks, specially made in Czechoslovakia, always travel in pairs, and the hoods of their engines are wrapped in quilted fabric. Once, when the temperature hit minus 76 degrees F, 150 trucks were stranded on the road to Magadan, their rubber tires split by cold. Cars have specially made double-paned windows, which prevent frost build up. Extra heaters are put in the space between the driver's seat and the passenger's seat. At minus 76 degrees F, car engines are left running twenty-four hours a day.

To imagine how cold it is, drink an icy frappe very quickly and imagine that aching pain in your head stretching all the way down to your toes. Be prepared for shutter speeds to slow down and brittle film to snap in your camera. Breathe inadvertently on the viewfinder and watch life through a foggy ice cube. Press your face against the camera long enough and your camera will be personalized with a piece of your skin.

People walk at a jogger's pace here. Blurs of fur stopping only briefly to blow out a frost-filled nostril.

Back inside the three doors of the Sunny Hotel, the woman behind the desk has a coat draped around her shoulders. She looks like a deep-sea diver trying to stay dry in leaky chambers.

In my suite the black cameras turn white. I try going back to bed with clothes and covers piled on. Still not enough warmth. So I write from the bathtub, where the hot water pipes are.

A cockroach shuffles across the floor. There are only two creatures that deserve to die—cockroaches and

The Whisper of Stars

Ust' Nera: A truck driver naps, his engine covered by quilting to protect it from the cold.

*Ust' Nera: A man climbs a mountain in the late afternoon, trying to
catch the last rays of warmth from the setting sun.*

The Whisper of Stars

mosquitoes. This Siberian cockroach is granted amnesty. If he can make it here, he can make it anywhere.

The mosquito has a short but bloody life in the Siberian summer. "Every summer we move the [reindeer] population north to the Arctic Ocean because the sea winds keep the mosquitoes at bay," says Nikolai Gabyshev.

"In July of 1972 the temperature changed dramatically from 5 [40 degrees F] to 20 [67 degrees F], and the mosquitoes appeared in big black clouds by the millions and billions, twenty-two days early," says Nikolai, his gold smile disappearing. "The deer were attacked. There was a black cloud around every one. The breeders put on [insect] repellent and tried lighting fires. The deer ran to the fires because they knew the smoke would help. We tried to move them quickly, but because of the babies we could move only five miles a day. The deer tried to run in circles because in the middle of the circle there were fewer mosquitoes.

"All the babies died first. The others got weak because they couldn't eat any grass. First a deer would wobble, then it would lie down and die. The meat was spoiled too. We tested it, and it had no blood in it. There were 15,000 deer. Twelve thousand of them died. We buried some of them in a mass grave with clouds of sea gulls circling in the sky. I never saw tough reindeer breeders cry before that day.

"I still remember the elk, fifty or sixty of them, standing in the Omolon River, totally submerged except for their nostrils sticking up into the air."

A helicopter ride to Omyakon is delayed one and a half hours because of fog. When we take off, I open a porthole window and begin to photograph the beautiful countryside. The cockpit door opens, and an Aeroflot crew member says photography is not permitted. Arkady says it is not permitted. I say we are paying $3,500 for this helicopter and there are no prisons or military bases out there. I see unspoiled snow-covered mountain ranges, and I want to show this beauty to my readers. "No pictures," says Aeroflot. "Not permitted," says Arkady.

On the flight to Omyakon an eyeball occasionally appears through a peephole in the cockpit door.

When we land I demand Arkady call Moscow for permission to take photos. He says it is not possible. Arkady calmly puts up with a torrent of words that he will never find in his English-Russian dictionary.

We are stopping to round up the usual suspects from the local soviet who know where the reindeer breeders are in the taiga. One huge man looks like he's on the card

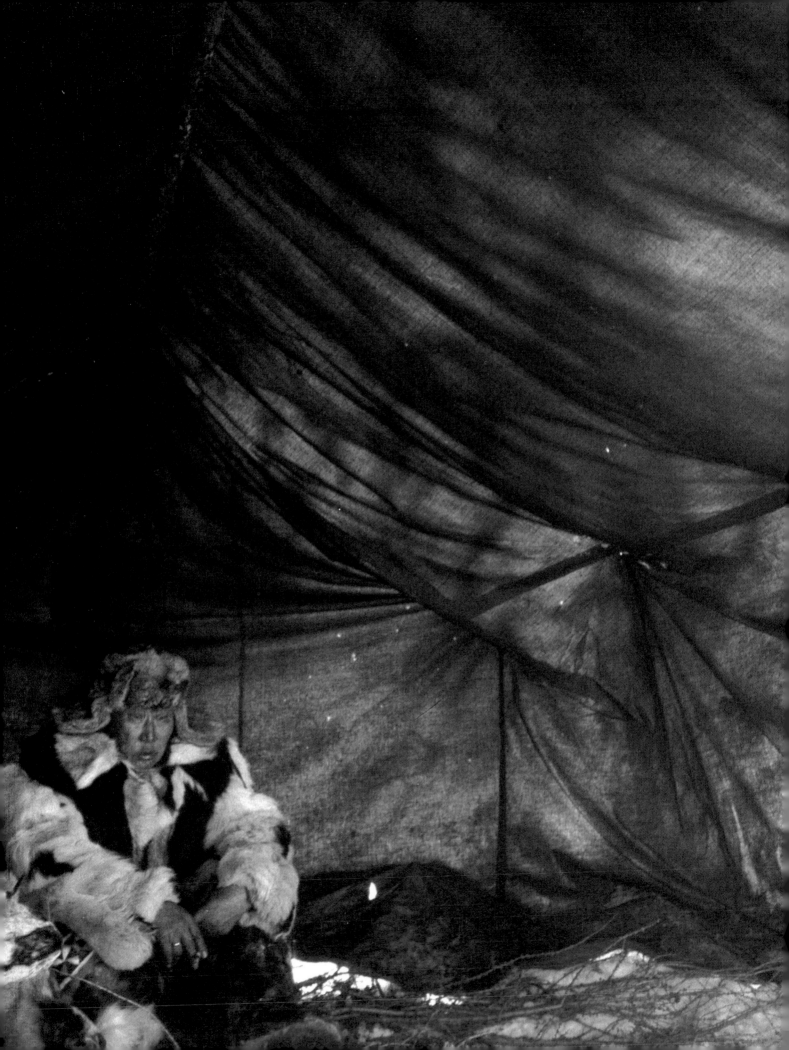

to wrestle Hulk Hogan at Madison Square Garden Saturday night. In my camera bag are British Airway blindfolds that were given out on the flight to London. I place them over my eyes, hold my wrists together, and announce that I am a prisoner in Siberia.

This stop in the taiga is supposed to take only fifty minutes, because the helicopter could ice up if we stayed any longer. I'm immediately placed on a sled towed by a snowmobile, and before I can get my gloves on (the custom of removing your gloves to shake hands holds true in Siberia despite the threat of frostbite) or my camera bag closed, I'm zooming across the taiga, my hands frozen, my cameras covered with snow.

The reindeer breeders live in a tent with a wood stove. Broken twigs serve as a floor, and animal furs keep them warm at night. They stay in one spot for two weeks, then move somewhere else. There are 380,000 reindeer in Yakutia, where reindeer breeding started. None of the reindeer are named Rudolph, or have any name, for that matter. The breeders say they are happy here. Siberia is their home. We dine on lean and tasty reindeer meat, washed down with piping hot tea.

On the way back to Omyakon by helicopter I see tracks in a valley, symmetrical patterns left by helicopter skis. I enquire about them and am told that geologists are working there. The snow-covered mountains and bare trees look like scoops of vanilla ice cream with chocolate sprinkles.

Yakut horses are raised to be eaten. Horsemeat is considered a delicacy here, as it is in Japan and France. The long-maned horses don't have to be fed, as they forage for food under the snow. Only in the spring when the foals are born do they need a little hay. Yakut breeders say they don't feel bad eating their horses. "The meat is best when they are young." The horses are killed by electrical shock.

The old-time herders remember receiving food from Americans who were delivering planes to the Soviets during World War Two. Unfortunately, they return the favor to me, bringing in chunks of frozen, uncooked horsemeat, which is fatty like bacon. They don't cook it or thaw it, but just dip it in a saucer of salt and eat it. The Yakut horseman Michail Gromov says, "If you want to live long, you must eat fresh frozen horsemeat, which will keep your organism warm during the winter." I politely put a chunk in my mouth and start to chew. I figure that if I hug the rail out of the gate, and maybe build up a furlong or two lead going into the stretch, I could get about two miles toward Belmont before freezing to death. Better to eat. . .

Omyakon: Snug in his tent and wearing a bulky reindeer coat, a hunter keeps warm seated on a floor of twigs.

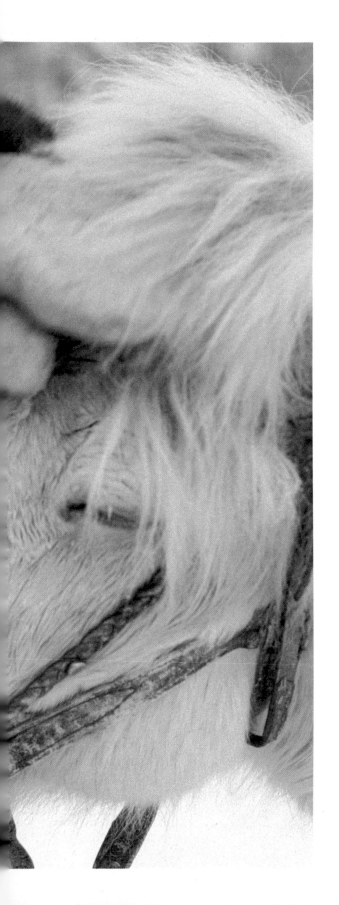

(above) Omyakon: Breeders round up the horses at day's end.
(left) Horse breeder shows affection for his animal

Omyakon: Siberian hunter and horse

The Yakut horsemen wear reindeer coats and boots. The boots are made from the leg fur of twelve reindeer. The pocketless fur coats sell in Yakutsk for $150. The horsemen object to my Gore-Tex coat. "It is not warm," says one. "It will bring cancer," says another. At 6:00 P.M. every day the electricity comes on. Lightbulbs are unnecessary in summer because the midnight sun shines sixty-eight days and nights.

The weather observatory in Omyakon is a log house. The forecast for the next couple of days is given in one word—"fine." The temperature reads minus 28 degrees F.

Maria Vinoktova, ninety-eight years old, remembers the day in 1933 when the temperature plunged to minus 96 degrees F. She is alert, active, and eager to tell her story. It takes time to hear it though, because it must be translated from her native language, Yakut, into Russian, and then into English.

"Earlier that week, some people died from frost in the taiga. We lived very poorly back then. The cows lived in one half of the log house; my mother, father, and I had the other. We knew it was very cold that day and very dark with the fog hanging to the ground like a cloud. We took turns getting wood outside. I only went out once, but just the act of breathing burned you like a fire."

Translating from Yakut to Russian is Mayor Varvard Zabolotskay. "When it hits 55 [minus 68 degrees F], school is cancelled for first to third graders," she said. Now, under bright sunny skies, the high temperature is minus 8 degrees F. Kids head out of school without coats on as nonchalantly as if they were heading for the beach. "We produce meat, milk, and butter by ourselves, and we are supplied well with apples and oranges. Our winter lasts nine months, and our summer is spent preparing for our winter."

An unscheduled stop in a local store reveals a good assortment of canned goods, candies, fresh apples— although small and bruised—and a huge block of butter. The mayor had said butter is produced here, but a box under the table reads "Butter—Product of Australia."

Later we are treated to such delicacies as frozen deer liver, which tastes a little like chocolate, *stroganina*, and *chokhon*, a chalky cookie-shaped frozen cream. Thank goodness some delicacies are only talked about. These include ground-up deer penis, believed to be an aphrodisiac by some cultures.

I am told about the Japanese who came here several years ago to film a commercial about a new kerosene heater capable of cooking spaghetti in the coldest place

Maria Vinoktova, a 98-year-old Yakut tribeswoman, recalls the day when the temperature fell to minus 96°F.

Varvard Zabolotskay, the mayor of Omyakon, translated for Maria Vinoktova.
(second overleaf) Omyakon: A sunset walk just outside the village, one of the coldest places on earth

in the world in two minutes. The bus broke down, the spaghetti froze into a log, the kerosene heater wouldn't work, and the Japanese had to be rescued.

The most popular place in new Omyakon is the sauna. There is something about being naked that makes a man more honest. Three Soviet men sit around and worry about war. One lost a father; another, an older brother; and the third, lost seven of nine brothers—all in World War Two. Kudrya says the United States entered the war two years too late. I remind him who landed at Normandy and who let the Russians march into Berlin first. Later, I will realize that our points of view reflect the way we've been brought up.

According to a *New York Times* article, Soviet textbooks castigate the United States for entering the war late. They downplay the action in the Pacific Theater, and they concentrate on the heroic Soviet effort and the battle of Stalingrad as the turning point of the war. American textbooks teach us about saving the Soviets with our lend-lease program and rescuing the Allies with the Normandy beach landings.

Alexander Grebenshchicov, who remembers eating dirt during the war, offers the figurative olive branch. "So we avoid war. We don't want it. We can't afford it. It is much better when Americans and Russians beat each other with birch branches than on the front lines."

A sign in Irkutsk said it best: "The unforgettable is not forgotten."

It is cold enough to make a wethead's hair freeze in seconds; but, sadly, it is not cold enough for the whisper of stars, which I have journeyed all this way to see.

The term is romantic; the reality can be deadly.

OMYAKON, March 20

It was back on March 8, 1986, the eve of the Women's Day celebration, a national holiday in the Soviet Union. The weather was "fine" by Siberian standards, a bitter minus 40 degrees F by mortal standards.

Valentina Kondakova, an eighteen-year-old Even artist, and Nina Atastyrova, a twenty-five-year-old Yakut medical assistant and mother of two, were visiting friends at a reindeer breeders' camp in the taiga. A car from town was supposed to come and pick them up before dark. The women became impatient and decided to start walking toward town. They had walked about three miles when the sun set and the cold rose. Valentina got tired, so they broke off some branches and started a fire.

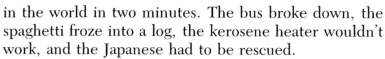

Siberians almost always carry matches with them, because in the taiga a match can make the difference between life and death.

They rested, hoping someone would see the flickering flame or they would see a pair of headlights. After a while, they started walking again. Valentina, who had a heart problem, fell. She wanted to stop, but Nina picked her up and carried her across her shoulders. They were lost, and now they could hear the whisper of stars because the temperature had dipped to minus 69 degrees F. To make matters worse, there were absolutely no faraway lights to head for, and all they could see were the milky clouds of their own breath. All they could hear was the *Shhhh, Shhhhh, Shhhushing* of the whisper of stars. The noise got louder as Nina labored harder with her friend's life on her shoulders. Now Nina was tiring. The handwriting was in the air. They stopped and made another fire.

"It's no use," Valentina said. "You're losing your strength. Go. Leave me by the fire or we'll both die. You have two children—perhaps I will survive until you bring back help." They hugged, and Nina headed away from the warm fire into the icy darkness.

She walked for many hours, trying to find her way back to the camp. She wanted to lie down, but she knew the rule taught to all Siberians when they are children. When it's below 58 degrees F, walk all the time, no rest.

It's too dangerous to rest, you just doze off and never wake up. First you lose the feeling in your fingers and toes, then your legs and arms. After one and a half hours, you will be dead. Those who have been found unconscious and have then been revived seem to have had the same peaceful dream. "Oh, it was so pleasant, so beautiful. I saw a lot of stars."

Nina had no strength left. As she trudged through the snow, her thoughts turned to her two children; and now, in the whisper of stars, she saw their faces. A boy and a

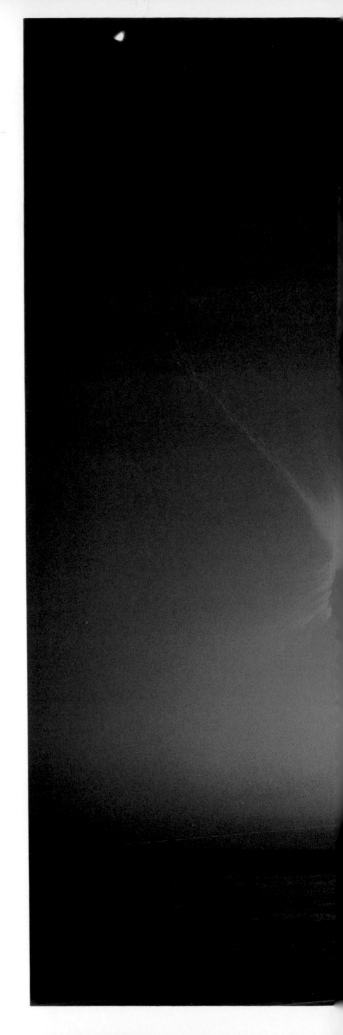

The Whisper of Stars

girl, ages three and four. *Shhhhh. Shhhh. Shhhhh.* With every breath she saw them in the icy crystals. The whisper of stars guided her safely back to the camp.

There is a teardrop that has been welling up in Arkady Kudrya's eye, and now it launches itself, pausing in the valley of his eye socket before racing down his cheek.

He ignores the tear and continues translating.

It was now the middle of the night, and the reindeer breeders retraced Nina's steps. The fire was out, and Valentina was dead. Her parents, reindeer breeders, aged rapidly after that night. In Siberia, too, a parent never recovers from the loss of a child.

MOSCOW, March 21

On the first day of spring, Arkady Kudrya and I return to Moscow.

It is almost 32 degrees F. The snow is melting in the sun, and birds are chirping. Because of the time change, the first day of spring will last thirty hours for me. The usual crowds are outside Lenin's tomb with the usual bouquets of flowers piled up. At the Tomb of the Unknown Soldier, still more flowers, including an arrangement of flowers from the people of Guatemala.

A Red Army soldier walks along with a red carnation in his hand. He is boyish looking and nervous. He is heading toward the Kremlin Wall, and I wonder if the carnation is for Lenin or the unknown soldier. But then he stops and waits, pacing back and forth. Within ten minutes he checks his watch five times. Finally a young lady in a leopard coat comes toward him. He steps forward, fumbles the flower, catches it softly, and presents it to her. She takes his arm and whispers something; together, they move slowly away from the Kremlin Wall.

Boston: Maya Plisetskaya, 62-year-old prima ballerina of the Bolshoi
Ballet, takes her curtain calls amidst the flowers tossed on stage.

Acknowledgments

These acknowledgments would look like a telephone directory if all the people who helped to produce this book were listed. If I forget a few names, please forgive me and realize that sometimes the best deeds go uncredited.

First, I would like to thank *The Boston Globe* and its readers for all the support and energy they have given me, and Executive Editor Jack Driscoll for sending me to Siberia—and then allowing me to return.

Managing Editor Tom Mulvoy always supports the stories I work on and always improves them. In an age where the public finds the media more and more suspect, he is a man of truth and justice. More importantly, he always signs my expense accounts on time.

A portion of this work first appeared in an expanded version of *The Boston Globe Magazine.*

A heartfelt thanks to Ande Zellman, *Boston Globe Magazine* editor, who allows you to be creative. She is a pleasure to work with, and her suggestions make this a better book. Louisa Williams, David Cohen, copy editors Elissa Rabellino and Elaine C. Ray, and layout editor Lucy Bartholomay all made this project memorable.

Vin Alabiso, *Globe* director of photography, helped edit the film. *Globe* co-ops Justine Schiavo and Judy Dragos did 3,653 chores cheerfully. The entire *Globe* photo department, as talented a bunch as any in the country, pitched in with support. Charlie Liftman and Sean Mullin deserve gold medals for their help in saving the text from computer-system monsters.

Linda Hunt, David Nyhan, Tom Winship, Sam Garcia, Kevin Lynch, Bruce Markot, Donald Brophy, Carolyn Threadgill, Charles Everitt and the Novosti Press Agency all made significant contributions.

Robin Young, writer, producer, and Life anchor at "USA Today"-TV, was more than generous in sharing her many talents. She is very special.

Mildred and Sandy Grossfeld monitored the progress of the trip across Siberia and were prepared at a moment's notice to perform a rescue mission. I love you both.

Technical Appendix

Page	Subject	Lens	f-Stop	Aperture	Film
Jacket	Siberian woman	85mm	f/5.6	1/125	100
Title	Sunset walk	24mm	f/8	1/2	100
vi	Soldier	135mm	f/2	1/90	200
vii–viii	Commuters	135mm	f/2	1/30	200
x–1	Tulips	85mm	f/5.6	1/125	64
2–3	War hero	18mm	f/16	1/8	200
4–5	Bolshoi opera	135mm	f/2	1/15	200
7	Swimmers	18mm	f/16	1/125	64
8–9	Kudrya	24mm	f/2.8	1/30	200
10–11	Food store	28mm	f/2.8	1/30	200
12–13	Bolshoi Theater	18mm	f/3.5	1/30	200
14–15	Statue	24mm	f/5.6	1/30	100
16–17	Olga	180mm	f/5.6	1/125	100
18	Subway	300mm	f/2.8	1/125	200
20–21	Father & Son	135mm	f/8	1/125	100
22–23	Airport	24mm	f/2.8	1/15	200
24–25	Novosibirsk	300mm	f/2.8	1/250	64
26	Stairs	180mm	f/5.6	1/250	100
27	Lenin statue	180mm	f/4	1/250	200
28	Smoking dancers	180mm	f/4	1/250	200
30	Young girl	18mm	f/3.5	1/15	200
30–31	*Swan Lake*	135mm	f/2.8	1/500	200
32	Fedor	85mm	f/2.8	1/60	64
33	Anastasiya	35mm	f/2.8	1/30	64
34	Siberian child	300mm	f/5.6	1/250	64
35	Sea swimmers	18mm	f/8	1/125	64
36	Fashion show	135mm	f/4	1/125	64
37	Snow	35mm	f/5.6	1/500	64
38	College girls	24mm	f/2	1/30	200
39	Boy with Lenin	28mm	f/2.8	1/60	200
41	Surgery	18mm	f/3.5	1/30	200
42–43	Tombstones	85mm	f/8	1/125	200
45	Foxhunting	300mm	f/2.8	1/500	200
46	Iced-in ship	18mm	f/16	1/8	64
48	Pointing hand	28mm	f/4	1/60	64
48	Guards	18mm	f/5.6	1/250	64
48–49	Eternal Flame	18mm	f/11	1/125	200
51	Young swimmers	300mm	f/5.6	1/125	200
52–53	Male dancer	180mm	f/2.8	1/250	100
54–55	Newlyweds	28mm	f/5.6	1/125	64
56–57	Market	180mm	f/4	1/250	64
58–59	Aboard plane	18mm	f/3.5	1/60	200
60–61	Ben Rubin	18mm	f/8	1/15	200
62	Making matzoh	18mm	f/5.6	1/60	200
63	Jew in prayer	28mm	f/11	1/15	200
65	Bear & child	135mm	f/4	1/250	64
66–67	Steam bath	18mm	f/8	1/60	200
68–69	Lake Baikal	28mm	f/16	1/125	64
70–71	Edik Kovyazin	28mm	f/11	1/8	200
72	Newborn baby	28mm	f/8	1/60	200
73	Twins	300mm	f/2.8	1/125	64
74	Children	28mm	f/8	1/125	64
76	Apricots	35mm	f/4	1/60	100
78–79	Clown	18mm	f/4	1/30	200
79	Circus fans	180mm	f/2.8	1/90	200
79	Fall from wire	85mm	f/1.8	1/125	200
80–81	Mother & child	18mm	f/3.5	1/60	64
82	Train	28mm	f/2.8	1/4	200
82–83	Victor	28mm	f/2.8	1/30	100
83	Star	300mm	f/4	1/500	64
84	Train picnic	18mm	f/4	1/30	64
87	Child	85mm	f/2	1/90	200
88–89	Siberian child	18mm	f/8	1/30	100
90	Ban the bomb	18mm	f/8	1/125	200
90–91	Hunter	135mm	f/11	1/90	64
92–93	Siberian house	28mm	f/2.8	1/2	200
94–95	Water carrier	18mm	f/5.6	1/125	200
96	School	135mm	f/2.8	1/125	200
96–97	Sweeping snow	28mm	f/2.8	1/30	200
98–99	Folk dance	135mm	f/2	1/250	200
100–101	Young boy	135mm	f/2	1/250	200
102–103	Two children	18mm	f/8	1/30	64
103	Frozen clothes	85mm	f/5.6	1/125	64
104	Fisherman	180mm	f/2.8	1/250	64
104	Fish	18mm	f/5.6	1/60	64
104	Net	18mm	f/5.6	1/60	64
105	Puppy	300mm	f/11	1/250	64
106–107	Girl in hat	180mm	f/5.6	1/250	64
108	Grain	18mm	f/5.6	1/125	200
108	Carrots	18mm	f/8	1/60	200
108–109	Pork	85mm	f/4	1/125	200
111	Medical student	135mm	f/2.8	1/125	200
112–113	Festival ride	300mm	f/2.8	1/500	64
114–115	Festival dance	400mm	f/3.5	1/500	64
116	Stilt houses	18mm	f/11	1/250	64
116–117	Pipes	400mm	f/16	1/125	64
118–119	Permafrost	18mm	f/11	1	64
120–121	Downtown	28mm	f/5.6	1/4	200
121	Fur hats	85mm	f/1.7	1/60	200
122–123	Sunken house	35mm	f/4	1/60	64
124	Indoor soccer	180mm	f/4	1/250	200
125	Pool triptych	85mm	f/2	1/250	200
126–127	Breeder	18mm	f/8	1/250	100
128	Three children	300mm	f/5.6	1/500	100
129	Mountains	135mm	f/5.6	1/1000	100
130	Truck	300mm	f/8	1/500	100
132–133	Climber	400mm	f/11	1/125	100
134	Hunter's tent	28mm	f/5.6	1/30	100
136–137	Man & horse	135mm	f/4	1/90	100
137	Horse pens	35mm	Autocamera		100
138	Hunter's face	18mm	f/11	1/60	100
139	Dark horse	18mm	f/5.6	1/60	200
140–141	Maria	24mm	f/5.6	1/60	100
142–143	Mayor	180mm	f/11	1/125	100
144–145	Star	35mm	f/8	1/8	200
146–147	Sunset walk	18mm	f/5.6	1/30	100
148–149	Maya	135mm	f/2.8	1/250	200